ENTREPEDIA

A STEP-BY-STEP GUIDE TO BECOMING AN ENTREPRENEUR IN INDIA.

by

Professor Nandini Vaidyanathan

ENTREPEDIA

A STEP-BY-STEP GUIDE TO BECOMING AN ENTREPRENEUR IN INDIA.

by
Professor Nandini Vaidyanathan

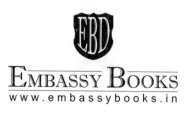

EMBASSY BOOKS
www.embassybooks.in

First Published in India: 2011

Published by:
EMBASSY BOOK DISTRIBUTORS
120, Great Western Building,
Maharashtra Chamber of Commerce Lane,
Fort, Mumbai-400 023, (India)
Tel : (+91-22) 22819546 / 32967415
email : info@embassybooks.in
Website: www.embassybooks.in

ISBN 13: 978-93-80227-81-8

Cover design and book layout: Namrata Chattaraj/WAG Design

Printed and Bound in India by
M/s. Decora Book Prints Pvt. Ltd., Mumbai

MENTEESPEAK

Life provides numerous ideas at various junctures; however our ignorance, mis-perceptions, self-doubt and a lack of guidance get the better of us. This book can transform the way we look at entrepreneurship! – Joydeep (CARMa mentee)

Every entrepreneur knows his business, he only needs someone to make him believe that. That someone is a mentor. – Bhavin (CARMa mentee)

This book captures the essence of 'starting up' and puts the key considerations on your radar. It tells you just what you need to know in simple, lucid and no-nonsense terms. – Marco (CARMa mentee)

A start-up in most senses is like a treasure hunt. A book like this can act as a blue-print or a map which an entrepreneur can customize to suit his needs to find his promised gold. – Anuroop (Startups mentee)

This book serves as a beacon of light to those who aspire to reach the pinnacles of entrepreneurship. – Sivabalan (CARMa mentee)

For existing and aspiring entrepreneurs a guide book for entrepreneurs becomes essential as it gives inputs on critical issues that as an entrepreneur we may overlook. It also gives an insight to aspiring entrepreneurs into the do's and don'ts of entrepreneurship and a realistic picture on what one can expect in the world of entrepreneurship. – Jaisinh (CARMa mentee)

A book like this will give entrepreneurs a realistic approach to setting up and running a business in India. Entrepreneurs need to be told up front the pitfalls and the rewards. Instead of going blind with only an idea, this book will fast track many entrepreneurs to achieve their goals quicker and will encourage many budding entrepreneurs to take the plunge as they now know how to go about it. – Gautam (CARMa mentee)

To dream is wonderful, the execution of which, is even better. A book like this will surely go a long way in giving wings to entrepreneurs who are

bursting with ideas. It will keep them grounded enough to help them fly. –
Ushma (CARMa mentee)

There's a lot to learn when you're starting a business for the first time. It's
more than you'll ever expect and more than anyone will tell you. A step by
step guide from someone who understands the industry is a great start to
get the ball rolling! – Lata (CARMa mentee)

TO YOU MEDINI, MY BABY
YOU STARTED OFF BY BEING MY REASON TO LIVE
YOU WENT ON TO INSPIRE ME TO LIVE THE WAY I DO
YOU WILL ALWAYS BE MY REASON

HOW CAN I THANK YOU GUYS ENOUGH !

First, all my students from across the world (15,000+) and my mentees (600 of them in both Startups and CARMa). Without you guys there was no meat for this book.

Nagesh – For introducing me to the magical world of entrepreneurship.

Varsha – For reaching out to me to write this book.

Sohin – For saying 'yes' to publishing it, so matter-of-factly.

Shabnam – For editing this book.

Rachna – My student, for creating such wonderful and appropriate illustrations.

Namrata– For the mind-blowing cover design and the unsual layout.

Marco – For solid inputs on Step 11 (he practically wrote it).

Abhijeet– For inputs on Step 6.

Ganesh –For giving me facts for both Step 9 and Step 12.

Mittal Saab and Aanchal – For cleaning up Step 9, by giving form and logical flow.

Hemant – For inputs on Step 18.

Vaishali – For her usual incisive inputs on Step 3.

Medini – For the whole thought process, structure and content in Step 15. For editing, subbing and formatting this book. And for digging appropriate quotations!

Shwetha – For suggesting the name, Entrepedia.

CARMa team – Hemant, Vaishali, Abhijeet, Kunal, Medini, Anil, and Prajwal – For giving me time off to wrap this book.

It's finally done guys!

And finally Appa – You would have been proud of me, if only you knew.

"WHY IS IT THAT THE HARDEST
THING IN THE WORLD IS TO CONVINCE
A BIRD THAT HE IS FREE, AND THAT
HE CAN PROVE IT FOR HIMSELF IF HE'D
JUST SPEND A LITTLE TIME PRACTISING ?"

- JONATHAN LIVINGSTON SEAGULL

HERE'S YOUR POCKET MENTOR!

This is not a textbook on entrepreneurship. This is my road map of the 20 steps that you need to take from the moment it hits you: "Omigod! Not being an entrepreneur is not an option at all!"

This is not a scholarly treatise on entrepreneurship either. I say this because I have no big bibliography to give you, although I have listed some of my favourite books at the end of this book. These books are not necessarily on entrepreneurship but they are books I would like to take with me on my journey to the hereafter. Don't be surprised if one day you see a book on entrepreneurship published from heaven!

This book is a ready reckoner for entrepreneurs in the start-up phase in India. If your starting point is a vague idea in your head that you want to become an entrepreneur, this book will guide you through the various steps you need to go to market with it. I did not pour over journals and books in the library to produce this. In fact, the entire book was on various flights! The 20 steps that I have discussed here are drawn from my own experience as a teacher of entrepreneurship and mentor.

For the last six years, I have been teaching entrepreneurship in engineering and business schools across the world. Each year, I teach over 2,500 students and they come from diverse backgrounds and they have different aspirations, mind-sets and goals.

For the last six years I have also mentored over 600 entrepreneurs, across domains and geographies, most of them in the start-up stage. Many of them came to me with just an idea in their head and today they are all running highly profitable businesses.

This book, therefore, is the result of my intense interaction with my students and mentees.

The first thing you will notice when you start reading is that the style of writing is conversational. It is as if I'm talking to all of you. A couple of my students who read the manuscript said they could picture me, standing in front of them, saying all of this in class – my gestures, my animated talking style and my pacing up and down in the classroom.

The language is very simple. I have steered clear of all jargon. The concepts are illustrated with a wide array of use cases, many of them drawn from my own mentee experience. I have also used a number of Indian examples because I do believe there is some very exciting work happening in the entrepreneurship space in India and not too many people know about it.

There are places in this book where I have used the expression 'my mentee' and there are other places where I have said 'our mentee'. 'My mentee' refers to all those 500 people, whom I mentored absolutely free, in my company Start-ups between 2006 and June 2010. 'Our mentee' refers to those whom we are currently mentoring in our company, CARMa, since July 2010, for a fee.

The steps in this book have been discussed in such a way that one leads to the other. This is not to say that you can't rearrange them. This is the way they flowed in my head and there was a logic and reason to it. But if you feel they can flow any other way too, feel free to jumble up the steps.

Whilst writing this book, I have tried to address most of the issues that pop up from concept stage to going- to-market. Inadvertently, I may have left something out that may be critical. If so, please do bring it to my notice and I will make sure we include it in the next edition.

One last word. I want this book to be your pocket mentor. What I would love to see is that it is on the bedside of every aspiring and practising entrepreneur, in every nook and cranny of India, dog-eared, heavily annotated, and looking every inch like it belongs in your life.

This is the reason I have kept the book thin. This is also the reason why we have priced the book so low.

I want this book to reach out to all of you who are bitten by the entrepreneurial bug, whether you are in a metro or a small mofussil town; whether you are an MBA from an ivy-league school or a high school drop-out; whether you speak accented English or are comfortable only in your mother tongue. This book will reach you shortly in many languages too so that not knowing English does not become a show-stopper.

Now you can't say, you want to become an entrepreneur, but don't know how!

THE TWENTY STEPS

LET'S START UP!

WHY SHOULD YOU BE AN ENTREPRENEUR TODAY?

"TALENT DOES WHAT IT CAN; GENIUS DOES WHAT IT MUST."

EDWARD GEORGE BULWER-LYTTON

I love telling stories, so it's only right I start this book with a story. You all know WalMart, right? This is a story told to me by one of its CEOs many years ago. This incident took place, when Sam Walton, the owner of WalMart, was alive.

A week before Christmas, their store in Denver was gearing up for the big Christmas sale. It had hired close to a hundred people in Sales and the HR Manager was exhausted. Just then a young sardar boy walked in saying he was looking for a job. The HR Manager said that he had just finished hiring and there was no vacancy.

But the boy was persistent and would not take no for an answer. That's when Sam Walton walked in and the boy went up to him and said, "Sir, I have just come from India and I need the job. I will come at whatever time you ask me to come tomorrow and I will work till I'm required to. At the end of the day if you are not happy with my performance, you don't have to pay me a cent. But please give me this one chance."

Walton perhaps saw some spark in the boy, so he asked him to report at 8.15 the next morning and work till 8.15 at night.

The next night Walton went in search of the boy and found him wrapping the shift up. So he asked him: "Young man, how was your day? How many sales did you make?" The boy diffidently replied: "It was ok. I made one sale."

Walton said: "On an average, each of our sales people makes 30-45 sales per shift. Just before Christmas, it is as high as 65-70. If you have managed to make only one sale pre-Christmas, you are obviously not good enough. I'm sorry but I don't think we can hire you."

Walton was about to walk away when something made him pause and ask: "What was the value of the sale?"

The boy replied: "One hundred thousand dollars."

Now it was Walton's turn to do a double-take. He asked the boy: "One hundred thousand dollars? What did you sell?"

The boy said, "Oh! A customer came in wanting to buy a small fishing hook, I sold him a set of large ones and some bait. Then I told him, 'Since you bought so much of fishing equipment, why don't you go upstream and catch some really big ones?'

The customer said that it was a very good idea but he didn't have a boat. So I told him, 'That is not a problem, we have a lovely boat and we can sell it to you.' Then I told him, 'Now that you have a boat, why don't you go to the woods that the river leads to and camp the night? We will even throw in some Budweiser free for you'.

The customer said he loved the idea, except that he did not have any camping equipment. So I told him not to worry, that we have some wonderful ones that we could sell him. He looked at all that he had shopped and said, 'I have done so much shopping, how will I carry all of this with me?' and I told him 'Don't you worry, we have an awesome 4X4 truck and we would be more than happy to sell it to you'."

Walton then asked him: "Are you seriously trying to tell me that a man came to buy fishing hook and you sold him a boat, camping equipment and a truck?"

The boy replied: "No sirjee, the customer came in saying he had a headache and wanted a pill for it. I told him fishing was a good way to get rid of the headache."

What was it this boy saw that the other hundred people in the store didn't?

Opportunity. The boy saw opportunity.

Did he only see opportunity? No, he also cashed on it.

Did he only cash on it? No, he even created it!

All around you today, opportunities are exploding like never before. The pace of change has been so rapid that it reminds me of what Pericles, the Greek philosopher said: 'The pace of change is so much that you can't step into the same river twice'. Cleon, Pericles' disciple, went one step further and said: 'The pace of change is so much that you can't step into the same river even once because by the time you have thought of putting your foot in water and you actually put it in, the water would have flowed'.

Just imagine what both Pericles and Cleon would have said had they lived today!

So what are the major drivers of change? Let's examine each one of them.

Technology

You all know what a huge change-driver this has been. During the 2007 Cricket World Cup, you could see, real-time, the entire match in animated form, ball by ball, on www.cricinfo.com. What made it possible? Technology! Two decades ago, if you wanted to be an entrepreneur, you needed at least 50 lakhs to put up a factory, buy machines and hire people. Even then, it took you 20 years to reach a turnover of ₹ 5 crores. That's why not too many of you became entrepreneurs.

But today, thanks to the internet, there are so many low-capital opportunities for entrepreneurs. I have mentored many internet entrepreneurs who have invested less than ₹ 500,000 and have had turnovers of ₹ 5 crores in 3 years' time. All thanks to technology.

Market shift

Which company invented the world's first transistor?

The answer is Sony.

Why did Sony invent the transistor? It was because the radio in those days was huge and bulky and you needed to remain by its side if you wanted to listen to news. So in that sense, the transistor made you mobile.

Who invented Walkman?

The answer is Sony again.

Why did Sony invent Walkman? Because Sony noticed that youngsters liked listening to music on the go, even when they were doing other things.

So who invented iPod?

The answer is, not Sony definitely!

Isn't it strange that a company like Sony, which understood the market need when it came to transistors and Walkman, failed to do so when it came to iPod? Isn't it even stranger that a company called Apple, which made computers and had nothing to do with the electronics entertainment industry, invented it successfully? Why did Apple see the opportunity whilst Sony and the others didn't?

The reason was simple. Sony and the others failed to spot the market shift.

When MP3 was launched, all the traditional music companies which were pretty much a mafia that controlled the entire music industry, went into denial. They said, digital music is a passing fad and people will come back to the old format.

Apple launched iTunes and a whole new industry was born where you no longer had to pay for music. You no longer had to listen to music the way music companies wanted you to listen. You could now 'download' music for free and the biggest freedom of them all, you could create your own playlist!

Do you know that more than 60% of the music downloads are as mobile ringtones? Do you also know which company is the largest retailer of music?

Airtel, a company which is a telecom service provider!

What made all of this possible? The answer is very simple. Market shift!

Globalization

This again has been a huge driver of change. Across the world, countries are encouraging cross-border movement of labor and capital; protectionist policies are being abandoned and trade barriers are being actively removed. The world is now emerging as one big market collective.

Besides removal of trade barriers, one of the most interesting features of globalization has been the realization that you may be a global brand, but your acceptance in economies other than your own is possible only if you adapt it to local culture. Let's look at some examples.

When MTV came to Asia for the first time more than a decade ago, it was with the assumption that young people like music and young people like the same kind of music, the world over. So they brought what was popular in the US market to Asia and expected it to fly. It didn't. It took MTV years of bleeding before they realized that the Asian youth's taste in music was very different from their US counterparts'. They then adapted it to local culture and very soon, MTV became an iconic brand in Asia.

The other day I went for a meal at KFC in Whitefield, Bangalore, and much to my horror I found this written on the menu: Dal Makhani and White Rice! That poor Colonel Sanders must be wondering whatever happened to his specialty fried chicken outlet! McAloo Tikki burgers, vegetarian Pizza Huts, and root beers in the Gulf, are all excellent examples of the emerging trends in "glocalization" – global brands, adapting to local cultures.

Government Policy

If the Indian Government had not changed its policy and allowed private players in telephony, you would still have had to wait for three years before your landline connection was sanctioned.

How many of you don't have mobiles today? It is hard to believe that just 15 years ago there were none in India because the government did not allow it.

Competition

The natural fall-out of globalization is that anyone from any part of the world can compete with you in your own backyard. Competition creates excellence in the industry, value enhancement for the customer and a robust innovation pipeline in the economy.

Let me share an interesting example with you.

Procter and Gamble launched Pampers in the Japanese market in 1972 and very soon it became a market leader. A Japanese company called Kao wanted to enter this market too but they were not sure whether they had the muscle power to take on the might of an MNC like P&G. So, like all Japanese companies, Kao decided to talk to Pampers' customers first to understand if there was an opportunity.

Pretty much all the mothers whom Kao spoke to, said Pampers was an amazing product and that it had made their lives so easy. It was disheartening for Kao but they persisted. Somewhere along the way, the first discordant note was struck. Some of the mothers said, whilst pampers was awesome in terms of absorption, it was a tad too bulky and made their baby's bottom look unnaturally big. Kao saw an opportunity here and went back to the drawing board. They created slim-trim Kao Merries, which gave them a 30% market-share soon after launch.

All of the above have driven phenomenal changes not just in India but across the globe. Each of them individually has thrown up an enviable basket of opportunities. In your generation you are lucky because they have all converged to create a staggering mountain of opportunities for entrepreneurs.

Now you may say: "Yes, I agree there are opportunities around me, but why should I be an entrepreneur?" Many of you will give me lots of excuses: "I'm too young", "I'm a girl", "I don't have work experience", "I don't have any money", "I'm not from a business family", "I don't have a business idea", "I know nothing about building an organization", and such.

My answer is: "Yes, these are challenges but they can be overcome. All you need to do is find yourself a mentor." (We'll talk about this in detail in Step 5.)

Given these opportunities, this is the best time to be in India. This is also the best time to be an Indian entrepreneur. So go take the plunge. You'll regret it for the rest of your life if you don't.

> TAKEAWAYS from 'Let's Start Up'

1. *We are surrounded by opportunities. The trick is not just in identifying and encashing them but in creating them too.*

2. *Technology, Market shift, Globalization, Government Policy and Competition have been the biggest drivers of change. Change in turn has thrown up a mountain of entrepreneurial opportunities. Be smart in spotting them before anyone else does, else your competitor will laugh his way to the bank.*

3. *This is the best time to be an entrepreneur in India.*

4. *Get a mentor to bridge your knowledge and experience gap*

WHY DO YOU WANT TO BECOME AN ENTREPRENEUR ?

" YOU CAN AVOID REALITY,
BUT YOU CANNOT AVOID THE
CONSEQUENCES
OF AVOIDING REALITY. "

- AYN RAND

This is the first question you need to ask yourself: "Why do I want to become an entrepreneur?"

In the last six years, I have mentored more than 600 entrepreneurs and I have heard all kinds of answers. Some are commonplace ones such as: "I want to make lots of money" or "I want to be my own boss".

Some are uncommon ones such as: "I want to create meaning in society" or "I want to define my identity".

Some are downright bizarre ones such as: "This is the only way I can avoid getting married" or "I can ask for dowry without feeling guilty".

Others, touching ones like this 67-year-old woman who came to me a few years ago saying: "I am pretty much illiterate; I'm also the wife of a very well-known industrialist. I want to become an entrepreneur because before I die I want to see respect for me in the eyes of my husband and two sons."

Let's analyze each of these excuses to dig deeper into what lies behind them.

I want to make lots of money

This is a bad starting point. Making money should not be the reason, but the result. If you start with this, chances are you will be so focused on making money that you will cut corners, compromise on the quality of customer experience that you will design, disregard good practices in organization-building and have scant respect for your team. All in all, it is a recipe for disaster.

On the contrary, if you do all the right things such as focus on putting together a team that shares your vision to design a never-before customer experience, a team who will create an organization they are all proud to be part of, one that competition benchmarks against and partners vie to be associated with, then the money will flow.

Money should be the unintended consequence of doing good in society.

There is also a flipside to this. Just the way some people want to become entrepreneurs to make money, there are others who stay away from becoming entrepreneurs because they think that they can make more money as employees. A student of mine told me that as a fresher he had an offer of ₹ 2.6 million per annum and he wasn't sure he would ever be able to earn that much in a his whole lifetime as an entrepreneur. The opportunity cost, he said, was very high and he couldn't afford it.

Clearly, the making-money-argument is not a good starting point for both who want to become entrepreneurs and those who stay away from it.

I want to be my own boss

I have heard this excuse the most often and the subtext here seems to be that if I am an entrepreneur I can do what I please, come to office whenever I choose, I have no one asking me probing questions, no one ticking me off when I haven't stuck to my deadline, and no one sacking me when I haven't delivered. In other words, being an entrepreneur means having untold, unlimited freedom.

This is a myth. As an employee you had one boss whom you had to manage, but as an entrepreneur you have several. And unlike when you are an employee, there is no one to shield you. You are at your most vulnerable. Let's see how.

"I can do what I please!"

Not really. Take, for instance, your product. There is no product if there is no customer. You may say, "I have designed my product the way I like it". But if your customer doesn't like it, you have two options – a) Change it to what your customer likes; or b) Go bankrupt. If we assume that going bankrupt is not your logical choice, then you have no option but to listen to your customer. And the way your customer holds the gun to your temple, he will make your nastiest boss look like Santa Claus!

"I can come to office whenever I choose!"

Sure. You also don't need to come to office at all because now you are working 24/7 from home, from holidays, from dates, from romantic candlelight dinners, even from your bathroom! As an employee, at least you had the luxury of carving some personal time in the day, distinct from office. Time you could call your own. As an entrepreneur, you are at the beck and call of your customer, round the clock. If you ever thought you were entitled to a personal life, as an entrepreneur you will quickly realize that the lines between personal and professional have disappeared.

"I have no one asking me probing questions!"

Says who? Look at this scenario. You haven't paid your team, so there is no question of your taking money out. You haven't let anyone in your team take a vacation, hence neither can you. When your team asked for a Diwali break, you shushed them and said, "Forget Diwali for the next two years till we go to market", so the same applies to you too. And god forbid if you have been funded.Not only will your investor probe into every aspect of your business but he will also tell you to how to run your business. He may even want to know how many times in a month you're having sex because it is cutting into your productive time at the office!

"No one to tick me off when I haven't stuck to my deadline!"

If you have ever taken a shouting from your customer, you will realize that your boss had actually washed his mouth with Dettol before he yelled at you! I always say this: becoming an entrepreneur is the best way to learn to appreciate even your worst boss! Your customer is not only sticky about the deadline he is also positively unforgiving and unreasonable about you not meeting it.

"No one can sack me when I haven't delivered!"

There is a beautiful English phrase popular amongst the British. It is called 'voting with your feet'. When you customer walks away from you into the loving arms of your competitor, he is voting you with his feet. In other words, he has sacked you as his service provider. And believe you me, this sacking can not only empty you of a job, but also of your self-esteem and your future. Your boss usually tries to sugar coat your sacking and will not tell you what a jerk you have been. But your customer will not mince words.

So there goes your theory that being your own boss means unlimited freedom!

I want to create 'meaning' in society

This is an excellent starting point. Being an entrepreneur means being unreasonable, being unbound, and in a sense, being selfish. What you're really saying is that I don't like the way my world is and I will change it. Reasonable people adapt to the world they are given; entrepreneurs adapt the world to their vision. In doing so, they create meaning in society and in creating this meaning, they make the world a better place.

The founding team of Mad Rat Games thought that children were losing creativity, thanks to the onslaught of Xboxes, and they figured that there was a need for board games in the Indian market to get them to think and create. One of the first products they created was a Scrabble board in Hindi so that children could still play Scrabble even if they didn't know English.

I want to define my identity

This is a good and not-so-good place to start. It is good to the extent that it is spurring you to action. But it is a very inward-looking approach to say that because I want to define my identity, I will thrust my ideas on you. If the approach is a combination of "I want to create meaning in society and in doing so define my identity", you have a winner.

This is the only way I can avoid getting married/I can now ask for dowry without feeling guilty

These are at best reasons that you can give when you want to impress your date or get a laugh out of your audience in a conference. The subtext in the first one is that no father will be interested in marrying his daughter to an entrepreneur and in the second, that it is good to marry a girl who may have buckteeth but brings green bucks to the marriage table. Really, there is no rocket science here, both lousy reasons any which way.

I want to see respect for me in the eyes of my people

This is a profound and far-reaching reason. The subtext here is,"I want to do something meaningful for which people will respect me and therefore remember me even after I'm long gone".

This brings to me to the reason why, knowingly or unknowingly, all of us want to become entrepreneurs. We may all articulate it differently, but the driving force behind our decision to become entrepreneurs is that we seek to leave a footprint behind. We seek to become immortal.

In the past we sought immortality through our sons. The Sanskrit word putra, which means son, comes from the word puth, which means hell. So putra means 'one who saves you from hell'. In other words, one who makes you immortal. Amongst Hindus, in the annual death ceremony, the son makes offerings not just to his father but to eight generations of his forefathers. This certainly is a clever way to be immortal!

Times and climes have changed. Now we seek immortality by becoming entrepreneurs. Again, look at this beautiful Sanskrit word, Antarprerna. It means "inspiration from within". That's who entrepreneurs are: inspired from within; magical thinkers. Entrepreneurs are like Prometheus, who stole fire from the fire gods! And look at this sheer coincidence – both words not only look similar but their pronunciation is similar too: Entrepreneur / Antarprerna!

This was the first step, defining the real reason why we want to become entrepreneurs. Now let's take the next step: convincing other people in our eco-system to buy into our decision.

> ## > TAKEAWAYS from step 1

1. *There are several wrong reasons to become an entrepreneur.*

2. *There are even more excuses to not become an entrepreneur.*

3. *But there is one compelling reason to become an entrepreneur and that is to transform lives!*

HOW DO YOU CONVINCE YOURSELF AND OTHERS IN YOUR ECOSYSTEM?

" WHY, JON, WHY?"
HIS MOTHER ASKED.
"WHY IS IT SO HARD TO BE LIKE
THE REST OF THE FLOCK, JON ? "

- JONATHAN LIVINGSTON SEAGULL

Your first step was to articulate why you wanted to be an entrepreneur. Next in line are two major challenges: The first, is convincing yourself that you should indeed become an entrepreneur in right earnest. The second, and a much harder challenge, is convincing people in your ecosystem – your family, friends, peers, bosses/faculty – that you are serious about becoming an entrepreneur.

So why is this step so important? Here's why:

1. Entrepreneurship is primarily all about emotion. The best of entrepreneurs envision with their heart and execute with their mind. One of our mentees is passionate about art and animation, being very good at drawing, herself. So she wants to create a world-class product that fuses both these domains together to delight her customers, way beyond their imagination. She's putting together a global team who bring not only competency to the table but also an enviable network and high-visibility connections. She's doing all this to ensure she goes to the global market with a next-in-class product.

2. There is also no such thing as the right time to become an entrepreneur. One of the things I am often asked is "What is the right age to be an entrepreneur?" My answer has always been that age has nothing to do with it. You become an entrepreneur when an idea grabs your imagination. It could be when you're 25 years old or it could be when you're on the wrong side of 40. Let the business idea be the driver for your decision, not age.

3. When you sit out of placements in your college to become an entrepreneur, emotionally it is the easiest on you. The biggest up-side is that you have not yet gotten used to a pay-check and the lifestyle that comes with that pay-check.

4. As you grow older and gain experience in working for other organizations, the decision becomes increasingly traumatic. Your generation is big on credit and plastic spending and your EMI's start literally from your first month's pay. So it is a tough and intensely emotional call to make — whether to become an entrepreneur and go

for a drastic lifestyle change or continue as an employee and remain in your comfort zone.

5. In India our entire identity revolves around our visiting card. If you have a visiting card that says 'Management Trainee, Oracle' it doesn't just define you. It's almost as if the brand equity of Oracle rubs off on you too, so much so people look at you with respect. On the other hand, if your visiting card says 'Managing Director, XYZ', people tend to be dismissive of you because your company is unknown, despite this exalted title. In my experience, it is this loss of identity that most of you find hardest to deal with, especially if you have worked in a well-known organization for some time.

6. During and post the dotcom boom, most internet entrepreneurs were in their early '20s. What they lacked by way of experience they made up abundantly by way of their obsession for creating innovative products. So much so that I have heard people in their early '40s lament that they missed the bus. In the last couple of years, I have seen this trend changing. In 2010, I was a mentor for and on the jury of 'The Economic Times' Power of Ideas' and much to my amazement I found that a significant number of the participants were in their early to mid-40s.

7. The upside of becoming an entrepreneur in your 20s is that your ideas and lifestyle are not yet calcified. You are still supple, flexible and mouldable. The down-side, of course, is that you lack organization-building experience, having never worked in one.

Conversely, the biggest up-side of becoming an entrepreneur when you are mature, having worked for several years, travelled, held P&L responsibilities, and well-networked, is that you tend not to make the usual mistakes young entrepreneurs are prone to. But the biggest down-side is that you have to pretend that you don't miss the corner office, the business-class travel, the exotic international family vacations, the high-power networking and the 'oh-i-have-arrived-and-it-feels-so-good' feeling that permeates your entire being.

8. Emotionally, the biggest challenge is the fear of failure. This is the one reason which stops many of you from becoming entrepreneurs. When you are in your 20s this fear takes on several forms:

- How can I repay my student loan if my business idea does not take off?

- What will my parents think of me if I fail?

- What will our relatives think of my parents? Will they taunt my parents that their son is a loser?

- Will I become 'unemployable' if my prospective employers find out that I am a failed entrepreneur?

- Will my friends think that since I failed in business they should stay away from me?

- Will it be hard for me to find a spouse?

- Will people point fingers at me and say that I'm a failure?

It is the social stigma that makes you weak and brings you down to your knees, not so much your economic losses.

All the above reasons are emotionally draining, and even more so when two or more of them combine. Each of them has to be carefully weighed, prioritized and addressed; not shoved under the carpet.

When you decide to become an entrepreneur, one of the best things to do is tell yourself that you have an equal chance of success and failure. Just the way you are mentally prepared for success, you should be emotionally prepared for failure as well. Look at yourself in the mirror and say that you will give it your best shot and if you fail, you will objectively analyze the reasons.

I have met a number of failed entrepreneurs and when I ask them why they failed, till date, not one has told me that it is because he didn't plan it right or he didn't hire the right people, or he didn't carefully listen to the customer or he didn't estimate the resources correctly or he didn't spend judiciously. It is always someone else's fault. The market crashed or customers were not ready or not enough money was there or the team didn't perform. Never once have I heard an entrepreneur say "My business failed because I failed to do the right things".

This, to my mind, is the most crucial emotional preparation that you need to make – telling yourself that, 'on the day of the reckoning, if I fail, I will be big enough to say, **I was the reason for it.**'

Once you have done this, it is easy to convince yourself that you should now become an entrepreneur.

The next and equally important step is to convince people in your ecosystem that firstly, you want to be an entrepreneur, and secondly, you want to be an entrepreneur for x, y and z reasons. It is my belief that if your reasons for becoming an entrepreneur are good, then you can convince others to see merit in your decision easily.

I have noticed some really interesting trends here. If your father is a businessman, chances are he will be against your becoming an entrepreneur. The reason is, when he started his business, not only were the opportunities limited but the government also was not pro entrepreneurs. That meant that your father experienced untold hardships, so much so, that when he sent you to an engineering or business school, it was with the sole objective of ensuring that you became an 'employee' in an MNC. Your decision to become an entrepreneur was never ever in his scheme of things. So when you announce to him that you are 'sitting out' of placements, his first reaction is one of complete shock followed by a sense of betrayal.

If your father has been an 'employee' all his life, chances are he will expect you to follow suit. His generation was short on cash and although they were not short on dreams, they put them aside so they could give their families a comfortable and secure life. Nothing you tell him as to why you want to be an entrepreneur will ever convince him that it is not just a passing fancy. The father of one of my mentees told me that just the way a new girl catches his son's fancy every once in a while, he was sure this 'bhooth' of entrepreneurship too would pass!

In both the cases, the only sensible thing to do is to sit your father down and explain why you are driven to becoming an entrepreneur, how your idea is a game-changing one and therefore with his blessings, how you will transform lives.

I also do believe that it is good to have naysayers in your ecosystem. This is what I call your 'hedgehog' network – people who will tell you that your idea will not work by ruthlessly poking holes in it. The more people tell you that your idea is doomed to fail, the better for you. So you can keep going back to the drawing board, tweak it and show them all how it can be made to work.

At the end of the day, no amount of explaining will convince people that you are on the right road. Carry all of them with you on the journey and show them how it works and slowly but surely they will all rally over to your side.

> **TAKEAWAYS from step 2**

1. *First convince yourself that becoming an entrepreneur is really what you want to do.*

2. *Avoid getting bogged down by the fear of failure – be prepared to face the brickbats just the way you were prepared to face the accolades.*

3. *It is unlikely that your ecosystem will understand your need to become an entrepreneur instantly. It's ok if they don't. Take them with you and show them how fruitful the entrepreneurial journey can be.*

STEP 3

WHERE DO YOU GET IDEAS FROM?

" IT'S KIND OF FUN TO DO
THE IMPOSSIBLE. "

- WALT DISNEY

In my entrepreneurship class, year after year, batch after batch, I always have one or two people asking me this question: "I like the idea of becoming an entrepreneur, but where will I get my ideas from? Is there something called an 'idea' bank?"

Unfortunately there isn't one. But there are opportunities for ideating, all around you. You just have to be smart enough to spot them before others do. Lots of people travelled in aircrafts ten years ago and many of them must have wished for air travel to be made cheaper so many more could fly. Whilst all of us just wished and sighed, one gentleman called Captain Gopinath introduced Indians to low-cost flying and opened up a whole new industry.

Let us look at a few opportunities for ideation. Mind you this list is hardly exhaustive, but merely representative.

1. Pain point

This could be your own or that of people around you. If it is your own, chances are you will go on complaining about it, even saying 'why doesn't someone do something about it', not realizing that, that someone could be you! Let me tell you a story to illustrate this.

Rahul moved to Bangalore from Delhi to join Infosys. It was his second job after engineering, and it was a job he had always dreamed of. It had good job content, excellent salary, amazing perks, and the opportunity to live and work in Bangalore. The icing on the cake was that he found himself a beautiful, well-furnished studio apartment, within walking distance from his office. For someone who was used to DDA apartments in Delhi, this well-designed apartment from a well-known builder set in artistically-landscaped gardens, seemed like manna from heaven. He quickly made himself at home, both in the apartment and in the city.

One week into his new job, he found the first irritant. His neighbor had a dog that wouldn't stop howling. At first, Rahul thought it was a one-off thing. But when the howling continued unabated, Rahul decided to do something about it. So one Saturday morning, he crossed the floor over to his neighbor.

His neighbor's door was open and he walked in, only to be greeted by an unusual sight. The neighbor was sitting on a chair, reading the day's newspaper and sipping tea. His dog was sitting right next to him and howling. The neighbor seemed completely oblivious to the howling dog and the howling dog seemed equally oblivious to both his master and the visitor.

Rahul asked the neighbor, "Is this your dog?" and the neighbor replied, "If you mean this guy who's howling next to me, yes, he's mine." So Rahul asked, "Why is he howling?" and the neighbor replied, "Because he's sitting on a nail." A shocked Rahul then asked, "Why doesn't he move away from the nail?" and the neighbor's surprising answer was, "He will, when it pains him enough!"

That is how it is with all of us. We will go on howling about things that trouble us. Many a time, we will wait for others to fix it, while only on some rare occasions, we may choose to do something about it. Let me give you examples of both.

a) Do something about your pain point:

A mentee of ours studied outside India for most part of the time and came home several months ago, looking for a job. He applied on all the usual job portals. Although he was extremely well-qualified in IT, much to his chagrin, he was either not getting interview calls at all or he was getting calls for totally unconnected jobs. After a month he decided to find out why, and to his horror, he found that there were several reasons for this mismatch.

Firstly, most existing job portals use keyword search to throw up results and if your resume does not carry those keywords, the search engine will not throw it up at all. For instance if your resume says, Java expert, but the keyword is Java programmer, your resume will not figure in the search result.

Secondly, since most recruiters who use the job portals for trawling are junior level people without much knowledge of the various terminologies, they would call him even if the job was not in his domain, based on some random word that was there in his resume. For example, if the resume said market analytics, they would call him for a marketing executive's role!

And lastly, all job portals use ancient technology which does not lend itself to advanced semantics. Hence search remains a futile exercise.

Armed with this knowledge, our mentee had two options. Crib about how job portals in India are terrible and wait for someone else to come up with a better portal or go ahead and design one himself that would address all these pain points. He chose to do the latter.

b) Wait for others to do something about your pain point:

You are stuck in a bad traffic snarl. The snarl is because it's a crossroad and vehicles are criss-crossing from all directions, without the discipline of giving way to others. You are late for your flight. Except for yelling at your driver that he should have taken a different route, you sit passively, without doing anything about it.

There is an old man in the car next to yours. He gets down from the car, walks up to the crossroad and starts controlling and directing traffic. Within seconds, the snarl eases and you are able to be on your way. Even as you speed away and you see the old man hobbling back to his car, you never ask yourself, why did it occur to him and not me?

2. Pleasure Point

My daughter's fiancé, Karan Karthik, is a passionate sound engineer, musician and a go-getting event organizer. He decided to combine all the three pleasure points in his company called The Live Gig, where they organize and produce musical events and also promote young musical talent. If you were to ask Karan why he thought of this idea, his answer will be: 'Because I wanted to make money from what gives me pleasure!'

The best thing about building a business around your pleasure point is it seems like all play, no work and actually getting paid for what you love the most!

3. Aspirational point

There is a very interesting lifestyle portal called tulleeho.com (a combination of the old hunting cry Tally Ho and the colloquial Hindi drinking word, tullee. Tullee is also supposed to be Indian for cheers!) Obviously as the name indicates, the site is everything about spirits – products, trends, news, places and the like.

Sometime ago, I received an invite from them to register for bartending classes, spread over some 12 weekends, at a cost of ₹17,000. I loved the idea and since I'm a registered member of this portal I thought this had aspirational appeal to many youngsters who have never known the finer side of imbibing alcohol. How many of us know what kind of glass to use for whisky, for instance? Or do we know the real difference between a wine tulip and a champagne flute? Do we know how to make great, innovative, mouth-watering cocktails? Or do we know what wine to serve with a particular cuisine? How many of us really know to 'enjoy' our alcohol? My point: An idea like this emerges from one's aspiration.

4. Situational

All the people living in Maharashtra, close to the sugarcane fields, have known for years that because of the distance between home and the fields, switching the irrigation systems on and off is something of a challenge. Everyone, including the farmers, has known it for years and it was pretty much on everyone's minds, but no one did anything about it till an entrepreneur in Mumbai called Santosh Jain decided to leverage the huge mobile user base to solve this problem. Result? Nano Ganesh – An application that sits on your mobile in the form of a button. With it, the farmers can now operate their irrigation systems without wasting energy, time, power and water. This solution was situational to the extent that prior to the advent of mobile telephony, and its popularity in India, it would not have been possible.

5. People first

Most of the times, entrepreneurs come up with an idea and then hire a team to create the product and build the business. William Hewlett, the co-founder of Hewlett Packard, had a different take on this altogether. His theory was that if you put good people together, they would create great products. "First who, then what" was how he articulated it.

Netscape is a good example of this. James Clark, the prodigious founder of Silicon Graphics (SGI), was unceremoniously ousted as Chairman by a man who was brought in by his investors. With fury and vengeance in his heart, he set out to look for someone he could partner with and create an organization that would make SGI look like a dime store.

After extensive search, he zeroed in on Marc Andreesson who had created Mosaic, the world's first browser that democratized the internet to all its users, the previous year. Andreesson, like Clark, had been wronged by National Center for Supercomputing Applications (NCSA) as it had hogged the limelight for creating Mosaic without giving any credit to its creator.

It was a strange partnership – Clark was pushing fifty and Andreesson was barely in his early twenties – but the two teamed up to revolutionize the internet by creating Netscape. Clearly 'first who, then what' works.

6. Idea Extension

All of you know that when mobile technology was new in India, you could go to your nearby mobile store and have your card recharged by using a scratch card, if you were a prepaid subscriber. EKo India, a company based in Delhi, extended this simple principle to bring mobile banking to rural India, so much so that they now have a network of more than a hundred thousand villagers operating their bank accounts through their mobiles.

7. Far-sightedness

In the late 1940s, Edwin Land had gone for a weekend vacation to the hills with his five-year-old daughter. Every time he clicked pictures of her, she ran up to him screaming: "Show me my picture, I want to see it". Every time Land had to explain to her that it was on a photographic film and that only after 36 exposures, he could give it for developing and printing and only after that could she see her pictures. But she kept asking: "Oh, but why can't I see it just now?"

And that made Land to think. Why can't we have a camera that produces instant pictures? He went on to invent one and the world knows it as Polaroid.

8. Cause-crusader

Sometimes, when you believe in something passionately and want to be the architect of transformation, you will not be daunted by the sheer magnitude of the task, or the absence of a precedent. You create your own way simply because the cause drives you. Naandi is one such example.

Naandi Foundation, one of the fastest growing social-sector organizations based in Hyderabad, was founded in 1998 with one objective: To make poverty, history in India.

Today, with Manoj Kumar as its CEO, Naandi feeds 1.2 million hungry children every day; provides safe drinking water to 3 million people in rural areas; runs 1726 schools guaranteeing quality education to over 100,000 children and works with 12,000 adivasi small farmers to export over a million kg of coffee every year. It is a B2G model where they convince governments to out source all these initiatives to them, for a fee. Their turnover – ₹ 100 crores!

9. Serendipity

Many times entrepreneurs come up with life-changing ideas accidentally. Here's one such example.

During the Great Depression of the 1930s, Earl Silas Tupper worked in a plastics factory in Leominster, Massachusetts. At the factory, there was a by-product, loosely called 'slag' which was nothing but an evil-smelling, greasy white petroleum waste. One day when he was fooling around with this waste, he discovered something quite remarkable. The slag could actually be converted into a nice translucent plastic which was not brittle, smelly or breakable. Most important, it did not lose shape and it did not react to heat or cold. He then went on to make kitchenware with it and today we know it as Tupperware!

10. Culture

Some of the best ideas in the world have been inspired by culture. A young couple in Mumbai in 2001, Dheeraj and Reeta Gupta, decided to create an iconic brand out of a local food fetish – vada paav. They applied the successful western fast food model to this immensely popular local snack food, and today, the company has grown to 43 outlets across India, serving over 40,000 customers in their outlets with a turnover of over ₹ 20 crores. We all know this brand as Jumbo King.

To sum up, opportunities to ideate are all around you. All you need is a hyperactive antenna that is sensitized to spotting such opportunities.

Toss around an array of such ideas, validate the opportunity each one presents, and choose a shark of an idea!

> TAKEAWAYS from step 3

1. *There is no such thing as a readymade 'idea bank' but if you look around, you will see a bank full of ideas.*

2. *Pain points, pleasure points, culture or even serendipity can lead to a path-breaking idea.*

3. *If you sit back and wait for someone else to come up with a solution, you just missed out on a lucrative business deal, my friend.*

STEP 4

HOW DO YOU CHOOSE YOUR CO-FOUNDERS?

" COMING TOGETHER IS A BEGINNING.
KEEPING TOGETHER IS PROGRESS.
WORKING TOGETHER IS SUCCESS. "

- HENRY FORD

This is perhaps as important as choosing the idea. Most entrepreneurs take this lightly in the sense that they do not apply much thought before choosing the founding team. So let's first talk about some myths and notions that surround this.

1. "We're best friends!"

I have heard this one, very often. Many youngsters tell me that they are a great founding team because they've known each other since school, they've hung out together for years, they even dated the same girl and basically they know each other inside out.

Whilst long association and familiarity are good parameters to go with, you should also remember that the two contexts are very different. The way you behave with each other as friends is not the way you are expected to behave as co-founders. The traits that look endearing in a friend may become the bone of contention in co-founders. Let me give you an example.

A mentee of mine from IIT Delhi got a taste of this recently. He and his co-founder came from the same small town in UP, were hostel-mates through engineering and decided to co-found a company in their final term. As friends, they were pretty similar-natured and fun-loving, intelligent and hard-working, loud and boisterous, with no steady relationships, and clearly they both wanted to breeze through life. In a way, they were compensating for the things they missed out on, growing up in a small town.

Given their similarity, it was logical that they co-found the company. Trouble began within six months. As the rigor of building the business grew, the intensity of engagement and the demands on the co-founders also grew geometrically. To add to their problems, they were even funded by a valley angel.

One of the co-founders figured early enough that their carefree days as students were over and that they needed to make an attitudinal shift, if they had to grow the business. So he decided to mend his ways but the other did not. Neither did he see the need, nor was he willing to see his co-founder's point of view. So the same traits which earlier were described as *bindaas* and *mast*, when they were friends, came to be seen as frivolous, superficial and flaky by the co-founder who was pushing for change.

Even before they completed one year, the co-founders broke up and the pity is that the one who stayed with the company hasn't managed to give traction to his business and the one who went away hasn't been able to start another enterprise.

This is also true of a husband-and-wife team. I have known a few couples who have managed to keep their bedrooms out of the office and have handled the challenges of straddling both worlds – being a couple and being co-founders – with incredible maturity. I have also seen a few couples who continue to be fantastic co-founders even after their marriages broke up. But I must say this: these are by far the exceptions and not the rule. I have seen more unsuccessful business partnerships and it is unfortunate that most often the wife opts out of the partnership, just so the marriage remains intact.

2. "We're both techies!"

Well, this is not something to crow about. Whilst it makes product-building robust, it does not make for great organization-building. I have seen start-ups with six co-founders – all of them coders! If everyone is engaged with the product, who will manage and grow the company?

Since resources are scarce, the typical tendency is to divide management roles randomly amongst themselves. This may not manifest as a problem in the start-up stage, but as the business traction demands competency and focus, the cracks will begin to show and it may actually become the show-stopper.

Ideally the co-founding team should have complementary skill sets. If there are two co-founders, in the ideal world, one should be a techie and the other, a finance or marketing whiz kid. It is important that there are plural competencies in the founding team, both in the early stage as well as in the growth phase. In the early stage, since there is not enough money to hire a finance or marketing guy, the co-founder who has that competency can drive the function single-handedly. In the growth phase, he will be able to do so with the help of a team.

In the event the co-founders have the same competency, it is important to recognize that whilst they may be good at product development, they need not necessarily be good at taking it to market or managing the company's finances. At this stage they should quickly bring in competent professionals to do so.

One of the things I have seen is that entrepreneurs tend to be possessive about their ideas and this possessiveness makes them believe that since they are the only ones who know how to develop the product, they are the only ones who can take it to market as well. Either they won't put together a competent team to execute, or even if they do, they won't give them a free hand to do it right. So even if the idea is brilliant, it won't spawn a great company.

3. "We have such a good product that it will sell by itself!"

This is the most notorious myth of them all. I have heard young entrepreneurs from ivy-league business schools say this. What they are saying is that they have a brilliant product but what I hear is that they don't need to build a team or that they can make-do with a mediocre team. This, to me, is the script of a horror story.

During the dotcom boom, the obsession was with the idea and primacy was given to it by investors without delving deep into either the composition of the founding team or its capability to execute. Post the dotcom bust, the one take away the stakeholder community has had is, that whilst idea is important, it is not everything.

There is a growing realization in the investing community that even if the idea is brilliant but the founding team is not robust, they should clearly stay away from investing in it. Conversely, even if the idea is a me-too, but the founding team is solid in terms of its passion, competency and purpose, it should be backed. A great team can build a great company with a mediocre idea, but a flaky team cannot do very much even with the most brilliant idea.

When entrepreneurs approach me for mentoring, I insist that they walk me through their vision. Many of them send me fancy PowerPoint presentations and expect me to be captivated by it. But I like to listen to the entrepreneur articulating his vision because I keenly look for nuances, those little tell-tale signs that show me how passionate he is about creating transformation. The words he uses, his gestures, and whether his body language matches his words — these are very important to me. So even if the entrepreneur is in a different location, I insist that we do a Skype call on webcam!

When I find that they all converge beautifully, my excitement builds. But if I find even one discordant note, I'm quick to pull up the entrepreneur on it. I tell my students and my mentees that having sat through so many business plan presentations and having mentored so many entrepreneurs over the years, my "bullshit" antenna is supremely sensitized and rarely do I miss that one little nugget that tells me that either the entrepreneur is not honest with me or there are other factors at play that is creating the dissonance.

4. "The larger the number of co-founders, the better!"

Not really. A good number is three, but it should not go beyond six. Three co-founders make for a good number because in the event the two hit a stalemate on some critical decision, the third can be called upon with the decisive vote. More than six founders may seem like overkill, especially in the start-up phase, unless they are able to hit the ground running from day one with an impressive portfolio of customers.

You should look at a founding team of at least three people if you are looking to raise early stage capital. Investors are reluctant to invest in teams with one founder. The reason is obvious. If you are alone, the risk is too much. What if someone invests in you and you die, or worse, you decide to pull the plug? If you are two of you, at least even if one wants to exit, the other can still be persuaded to continue.

5. "We don't need to do any documentation as we trust each other completely!"

I have learnt one thing in all these years. In business, there are no friendships. There are only interests. And selfish ones at that.

When you start off with an idea, all you have is a dream, and a sense of adventure. Not having money is the most romantic thing in the world, at that stage. You're waiting for the day you make your first million so you can tell the world how you and your friend started the business with ₹ 10,000 that you both managed to scrounge from your pocket money. It's heady stuff. And just imagining it gives you goose bumps. So the last thing on your mind is documenting the terms and conditions of your partnership. Some of the foolish things you do are:

- *50:50 share-holding between two co-founders:*

  This is not recommended at all. If it is two of you, it is always good to do 51:49. One person should always have a majority share-holding stake, at least in the early stages. The person who keeps 51% is typically the guy whose idea it is or whose responsibility it is to develop the product. This is important from the point of view of driving certain crucial decisions.

- *Not clearly spelling out what the responsibilities of the co-founders are:*

  The assumption is that all the co-founders are responsible for everything. While theoretically this sounds good, in practice, nothing can be more disastrous than this.

  It is good to identify roles and responsibilities based on competencies right from day one and document it. A mentee of mine actually created job descriptions for all the four co-founders along with the business plan, including key result areas on which their performances were to be evaluated. This worked wonders because there was no ambiguity in terms of what roles they were expected to play, what their responsibilities were and what their deliverables were. It kept them on their toes and it sent a very clear signal to the hired team that there were no free lunches even for the co-founders.

- *We are the co-founders and so we don't have to be evaluated:*

Says who? Co-founders, if anything, are more accountable, therefore, there is a greater need to make sure they perform. A mentee of mine introduced a 360-degree evaluation for the entire team including the co-founding team. This meant each employee was rated by his boss, subordinate and peers. This in turn became the basis for up-skilling people in the team.

If there is no evaluation, how do you know when and how to invest in yourself? I have seen entrepreneurs spending big bucks on bringing their teams up to speed by sending them to conferences, organizing training interventions, and even letting them enrol in specialized courses. But they seem to think that they are exempt from all of this. The result is that as the organization grows, the team also grows, but the founding team remains where it is and becomes the show-stopper.

A 360-degree evaluation across the organization sends excellent signals down the line, that everyone has to be in the driver's seat, that passengers are not encouraged, that there is a level of transparency which is extremely inviting, and that the company is on its way to becoming a great organization. The best lessons are those that are learned from bosses who lead by example. I have heard that on many an occasion, Narayan Murthy is seen picking up a cigarette stub from the cobbled paths along the garden and dropping it off into the dumpster.

What better way to teach teams that keeping their work areas clean is everyone's responsibility?

6. "We will be together, forever!"

Remember the old English proverb, 'the road to hell is paved with good intentions'? Just the way there is a 50:50 probability that you will succeed when you start a new business, there is that same probability with the founding team. The team may work and deliver beautifully or it may not deliver and fall apart.

Let's say you are two co-founders. Let's say only one is a domain expert and the other is a marketing guy. In the early phase, the dependence on the domain guy is phenomenal. Suppose even after two years there is no product. What does the other guy do? He should be able to take a call to kick the domain guy out of the partnership.

If you have documented this possibility and put a value to it right at the beginning, it makes the disruption easier. If you haven't, the breakup can get really nasty. It is always good to factor in such an eventuality right at the beginning of the partnership and put a metric in place as to how the exit process will happen.

One of our mentees had a strange encounter. They were a four-member founding team and pretty early on, they found that one of them was not contributing, so they decided to push for the exit of that person even before revenues kicked in. To their horror they found that he wanted an unreasonably fancy amount before he exited!

Founding teams foster organization culture

A good founding team builds a great organization. Let's not forget that the organization is built on the values that the founding team brings to it. Organization culture is nothing but the team's shared ways of thinking and doing. Values are integral to it.

Culture is top-down in the start-up stage and bottom-up, as the organization grows. It is the founding team that sets the value framework and it is internalized well throughout the organization only when the founding team shares the values and demonstrates its commitment by practising it consistently, without exception. A value-fit amongst co-founders is a non-negotiable item.

A mentee of mine had an interesting dilemma a couple of years ago. Very early on, his company had formulated a policy that intra-team dating and marriage would not be encouraged. Unfortunately, one of the co-founders fell in love with his software architect.

The issue came up for discussion on the company's blog. The general consensus was that it was a good policy to have for the hired teams, but maybe an exception can be made for the founding team. My mentee and I had long discussions on this and I pointed out to him that even though the teams had given him the thumbs up, it would significantly weaken his position as a leader if he went ahead with it. After much angst-ridden deliberation, he decided that he will not marry her and jeopardise his stature as leader. The fact that he chose this moral high ground has earned him the respect of his entire stakeholder community.

Equally important is the fact that co-founders share the vision. A mentee of mine had very serious issues with his co-founder because whilst he wanted to take it slow and do it right, his co-founder was in a hurry to see results and in pursuit of that, he did not mind cutting a corner or two. This cause endless arguments between them.

Another mentee of mine had a partner who loved saying: "We are in the business for the long term" and as an extension of this, only focused on long-term results. I had to sit him down several times to impress upon him that 'there is no long term without the short term!'

Remember one thing, choosing the right co-founder is crucial not only for building the business but it also has long term implications for you and the business. So dwell on it, do all the due diligence needed, do all the necessary documentation to safeguard the business interests and then go for it.

When should co-founders come together?

This is a question I'm often asked. Is it right at the beginning, in the ideation stage? Is it after you have created the product and are ready to go to market? Is it when you're looking to raise early capital? There is no formula answer. The simple and commonsensical answer is, when you find the right person. Just because you can't get funded if you are single, don't be in a hurry to shop and pick up the first person who comes along the way.

> ### > TAKEAWAYS from step 4
>
> 1. *Value-fit is absolutely important at any stage while picking a co-founder.*
>
> 2. *Similar demographic backgrounds help.*
>
> 3. *In the start-up stage, decide on how much capital both of you will bring to the table and the stake should be a function of that.*
>
> 4. *In the growth phase, don't do stupid things like offering sweat equity (i.e. he brings in only experience and no capital to the table) or valuation at par.*
>
> 5. *Like for everything else, get yourself a good mentor who will help you take the right decisions.*

STEP 5

WHO IS A MENTOR AND WHY DO YOU NEED HIM?

" NOTHING IN THE WORLD IS MORE DANGEROUS THAN SINCERE IGNORANCE AND CONSCIENTIOUS STUPIDITY. "

- MARTIN LUTHER KING JR

Who is a Mentor?

Two questions aspiring entrepreneurs invariably ask me are: Who is a mentor and where can I find him? We'll address both these questions in this step.

Can anyone who gives me advice be called a mentor?

No. There is no dearth of people who will give you advice. But all of them are not mentors. Mentors are those who handhold you to make sure that the advice they give you is a call for action. So it is advice with accountability.

What can I expect from my mentor?

A mentor brings to the table, three mission-critical things: Firstly, he brings his experience. This is absolutely necessary because when you are fresh out of college, you don't know what an organization looks like, so left to yourself, you may arrive at a successful blueprint only after a lot of trial and error. A mentor with experience can bridge this gap and save you time, money, effort and heartache.

Secondly, a mentor opens doors for you which may otherwise remain shut. A mentor is someone who is very well-networked and has credibility in his habitat. Networking may be for bringing in other mentors, for gaining market access, for validating a business idea, for raising capital or for developing the product. In other words, for just about anything.

Thirdly, a mentor is your mirror. He is expected to tell you things exactly as they are, not sugar-coat them. He's not the devil's advocate, he is the devil himself.

Should the mentor know everything that there is to know?

Now you're being unreasonable. A mentor is not Buddha and you are not his disciple. If you have a mentor to help you with business strategy, it is not even necessary that he knows your domain. A good mentor is one who has organization-building capabilities. Even if he doesn't know your domain, he should have the perspective to point you in the right direction.

Can I have more than one mentor?

Of course yes. If you are one of those lucky guys, more power to you! You can have a mentor in your domain for product development, you may have another one for going-to-market, and you may have a third, for financial structuring.

How do I pay the mentor?

This is an arrangement between you and your mentor. Some mentors charge a small monthly retainer fee against which they provide mentoring and this may be articulated in the terms of engagement. Some may ask for sweat equity in your company, typically up to 5%. Others may invest in your company for a 10% stake and mentor you. Some may even charge an up front, one-time fee. The models are many and may be tweaked depending on mentor-and-mentee convenience.

We at CARMa have a unique model. We offer a 6-month intense mentorship program called CARMa Sutra. The reason behind a 6-month program is that it is possible to demonstrate, in that time, how milestones can be reached.

You may be a start-up, a mature enterprise or a family business. We ask you to identify three areas where you want to be mentored. If we leave it open-ended, it will become a rambling wish-list with no clear action-focus. The three areas may be your most vulnerable areas or your priority ones. For example, you may say, "I'm great at developing product but I am not commercially savvy so I need a mentor for my go-to-market strategy". Or you may say, "Getting my product right is critical to the success of my business and I can't afford to not have a mentor for product development".

Once you identify your three areas, they go into Scope of Mentoring in our Mentorship Agreement. The scope is further broken down into milestones so that the mentor and mentee can set tasks for reaching them.

One main mentor is assigned to drive the engagement. Like I said earlier, he may not be a domain expert but he should certainly have the ability to align your tasks, actions and strategies to your milestones which in turn is aligned to your vision.

The main mentor may bring in other mentors from time to time. For example, he may bring in someone with financial acumen to make sure that you incorporate all good corporate governance practices within your organization. He may bring in a domain expert to make sure that you have a clear value offering to your customer. So typically, in a 6-month program, you will have exposure to at least three or four mentors.

The biggest advantage of this to you is that each mentor not only brings his skill and experience to the table, but also brings the benefit of his network to you. As you know, the two biggest pain points for all of you is access to resources and markets. And this is exactly what we address in CARMa. CARMa is an acronym for Creating Access to Resources and Markets.

For enrolling in CARMa Sutra, we charge a nominal one-time mentoring fee, upfront, for the whole duration.

How can I trust my mentor?

You trust your mentor exactly the same way you learn to trust other people in your eco-system, such as employees, customers, and partners. You do adequate due-diligence, you establish his credentials, you talk to other people whom he has mentored, and you establish proof of concept. Finally, go with your gut feel. It is very important that you connect with your mentor at a basic human level. Both of you need to like and respect each other, first as human beings and then as professionals.

This brings us to the second question.

Where will I find my mentor?

You won't find him with a doggie tag that says Mentor! Mentors are hidden gems and you need to dig them out. But look around you – there is enough and more activity happening, at least in the metros in India.

There are lots of people today who are passionate not just about creating entrepreneurs, but fostering an entrepreneurial economy in India. Dig them out from the pages of LinkedIn, from the lecterns of a TiE conference, from the blogs of holykaw.com, from TED talks, from a casual conversation in a waiting room, from an event at Headstart or Proto or OCC, from the incubators in engineering and business schools. In other words, from just about anywhere. Just the way you look out for opportunities, look out for mentors too. Seek and thou shalt find!

Is a mentor the same as a coach or a consultant?

When people ask me what I do for a living, I say, I teach entrepreneurship and mentor entrepreneurs. "Ah!" they say, "So you're a consultant". Politely I say, "No, I'm not". Promptly comes the next question: "So you're a coach?" Again I say, "No, I'm not". Most people give up at this stage thinking I'm unnecessarily quibbling. But the persistent ones comment, "It's the same thing, no? Isn't a mentor the same as a consultant or a coach?"

No, no and a very big no. Let's look at some key differences.

● **Focus**

Consultant: The focus area for a consultant is a billable engagement. The emphasis is on the process and not on the outcome. For example, a consultant may be retained to put processes to monitor and track sales leads. He will do this by getting the workflow in place, plugging the leaks, and devising a tracker. But generating sales leads that lead to conversion is not his focus area at all.

Coach: The focus area is performance. Wily nily, he has to make sure that the team or the person he is coaching delivers in the given period. But capacity-building to sustain delivery is not his focus area at all.

Mentor: The focus area is robust capacity-building. A mentor is a combination of a teacher and a coach. He will share knowledge with his mentee like a teacher, up-skill him constantly, and get him to deliver like a coach, not once, but time and time again.

- **Key skills**

Consultant: He will tell you very clearly what is wrong and why. He will also very clearly tell you what should be done to right the wrong. Rarely is it his mandate to hand-hold the client to actually do it.

Coach: He gives ruthless feedback on performance but does not see it as his responsibility to pre-empt the outcome.

Mentor: He is a blend of a counselor and a teacher. He listens, questions, explains, and in so doing, gets the mentee to discover his potential and come up with solutions.

- **Orientation to goal**

Consultant: Since he's more focused on the process, that in itself becomes the goal.

Coach: He sets or suggests goals which should be pursued.

Mentor: His starting points are his mentee's goals. He mentors him to align his task and strategies to the goals that he has set for himself and his organization.

- **Type of relationship**

Consultant: Formal, more distant than close, low intensity.

Coach: Formal, more close than distant, moderate intensity.

Mentor: Informal, extremely close, very high intensity.

- **Learning engagement**

Consultant: One-way – from the consultant to the client. The approach is: I know more than you do, do as I tell you, especially since you're paying me for it.

Coach: One way – from coach to his ward. The approach is: Don't question what I ask you to do.

<u>Mentor:</u> Two-way learning process. The mentor does not have all the answers and is quick to tell that to his mentee. The attitude is one of: Let's both learn along the way.

To me, a mentor is someone who bridges the experience gap, who opens doors and who hand-holds with accountability and responsibility. The mentor and his mentee are both on the same side; they share the same vision, and have the same passion for changing lives. Most importantly, a mentor is someone who never says 'your company' to his mentee. He always says 'our company'.

> TAKEAWAYS from step 5

1. *Everyone who gives you advice is not a mentor.*

2. *Mentors are rare but not impossible to find if you just look in the right places.*

3. *Don't be unreasonable in your expectations of your mentor. He doesn't have all the answers, but he will find the right people to find those answers.*

4. *A mentor is not the same as a coach or a consultant or a teacher or a counselor. He is a breed in himself!*

5. *Remember, the mentor is always on your side. But if he has to take sides, he will choose the interest of of your organization over you.*

This chapter is reprinted with permission from two separate articles published in the entrepreneur magazine.

STEP 6

HOW DO YOU ESTIMATE RESOURCES FOR YOUR BUSINESS?

"DON'T STAY IN BED, UNLESS YOU CAN MAKE MONEY IN BED."

- GEORGE BURNS

Now that you have found yourself a mentor, it is a good time to plan your resource requirement for the next one year. The next three steps that you take are all intricately linked with each other – estimating your costs, building a robust revenue model (covered later in this step) and crafting the business plan (step 7).

Why is it important to know what your costs are likely to be? It is, for two reasons really. Firstly, it gives you an idea about how much capital you need to raise to meet those expenses. Secondly, it helps you micro-manage your expenses. Thirdly it also tells you very definitively when you can expect your revenues from sale.

If you were to analyze why the mortality rate for start-ups is so high—in the first year of operation (80% of them shut shop within the first year), you will find that the biggest culprit is money. Rather, lack of it. When you don't estimate expenses correctly, you obviously can't plan properly. So chances are, you will run out of steam much earlier than you thought.

I always tell our mentees, raise money when you don't need it because you can then negotiate from a position of strength. If you try to raise money when you have a huge bill to pay and no cash, you will do stupid things to raise money, like sell equity to the wrong people, sell it at the lowest valuation, hire incompetent people just because they are available cheap, compromise on quality of product, delivery, and promise and cut corners in everything that you do. You will also do unethical things like not filing for your taxes or maintaining number 2 accounts or flouting safety laws.

All this will prove expensive in the long term.

A start-up is like a perpetually hungry baby and demands constant feeding (cash). If you don't plan for every feed properly, you will starve the baby. A starved baby is a kill joy not only for you but also for everyone connected with you.

Estimating resources means that you do the following things:

- Identify all your heads of expenses.

- Identify the periodicity of their payout.
- Calculate how long you will have to manage before revenues kick in.
- Total up all the expenses till revenues accrue (give yourself a realistic margin for error).
- Identify sources from where you can raise money to meet all these expenses.
- Identify multiple revenue streams.
- Plan for cash flow.
- Plan for contingencies.

Now, let's understand each of them.

- **Heads of expenses**

Expense is the same as cost. It means that you have to pay someone for a service they have rendered to you.

Typically, there are direct and indirect costs.

Direct costs are those which have gone into creating your product. For example, if your product is a watch, the cost of all the parts that have gone into it, the steel that you have used for its body, the leather strap, the labor for making the watch, the design, etc. are all direct costs.

Indirect costs are, the cost of the factory where the watch was made, the electricity and water, telephone, internet, fax and other communication used, transport of raw material into the factory and transport of the watch from factory to the market, management cost, cost of financing the whole operation, stationery, marketing, branding etc.

Let's look at some of the major direct and indirect costs in the start-up phase, and how to keep them low:

1. <u>Product Development Cost</u>: After you have zeroed in on the idea, you need to check the market-acceptability of your product. You need to talk to your potential customers to find out whether they will buy your

product. After taking inputs from them, you will build the first prototype. You will need to put time, effort and resources to build it. You will then showcase it to your customers, take their feedback, and based on that, improve it yet again.

2. Marketing Cost: Most of you feel that you have a world-class product, and therefore it will automatically sell. Rarely does such a thing happen. You need to tell people about your product. Thanks to social media, your marketing cost can be significantly reduced (see Step 16). I know of many start-ups that get people to write about their product/service in blogs, media forums and newspapers.

3. Training and Seminar Cost: You need to attend seminars related to your business to understand what is happening in your industry, build new contacts and get inputs from people. You also need to identify a mentor who can guide you and give you different perspectives on different ways of doing things. A good mentor doesn't come free! (As you saw in Step 5.)

4. Operational Cost: I will break this up into the following sub-headings:

   a. Manufacturing cost: If you are manufacturing the product, you will need to buy raw materials, hold inventory, store finished product, etc.

   b. Infrastructure cost: This includes manufacturing facility/office, power and water, communication, canteen/pantry.

   c. Salaries: You will need to pay your employees. You may not take a salary, but you need to factor it in your book of accounts.

   d. Travel: You won't realize how much you will need to travel to understand your market, your customers, for networking at seminars, etc. All of this costs a lot of money.

   e. Legal and Accounting Cost: You will need to hire a Chartered Accountant / Lawyer to incorporate your company, file for your patent, handle your book-keeping and statutory compliance etc.

5. <u>Technology Cost:</u> You need technology for your product development, you may need software licenses, you may need to invest in hardware not just for IT, but production as well. You will also need a good website to showcase your business to the world. There are one-time website-development costs and ongoing maintenance costs.

   ✓ Simple but effective ways to reduce your costs:

   ✓ Free tools for communication: Use Skype (for conference calling) and

   ✓ TeamViewer (for desktop sharing) for communication.

   ✓ Help from friends: You will need lawyers, accountants and coders for your work and it is good to ask your friends for reference.

   ✓ Freelancers and interns: Don't look at hiring people full time; instead look for freelancers and interns.

   ✓ Social Media: Use Facebook, LinkedIn and Twitter to reach all your stakeholders. Check how 'Khan Chacha' and 'Wildcraft' are attracting people to their Facebook page and increasing their sales. You should also look at writing blogs to acquire customers as well as to get their feedback. Also advertise your products and company on different free ad sites such as www.clickindia.com (see Step 16 on how to use social media tools for marketing).

   ✓ Build Partnerships: Invest in building partnerships with your customers, your suppliers and others in your habitat.

● **Periodicity of payout**

This is important from the point of view of cash flow. Salaries, for example, have to be paid on a stipulated day at the end of the month. Rent has to be paid a month in advance. Transporters may be paid once in two months. Interest on loan has to be paid every quarter. Identifying when to pay each bill of expense helps you make provision for it. It is also a healthy management practice so you don't get a reputation in the market that you are slack with your payments.

● **Planning**

You also have to plan your schedule for going-to-market, which depends on when your product will be ready. Even the best laid plans go awry because you all underestimate the time it takes for market readiness. Be realistic. If your gut says your product needs six months to be developed, plan for a buffer of at least three more months. Stick a Gantt chart where the whole team can see it and do the countdown religiously. Keep reviewing and updating the schedule every single day so, at any given point in time, you know whether you are on track or not.

● **Source of fund**

There is a huge time lag between starting your company and going-to-market. All the product development and management expenses have to be met with, till you acquire paying customers. So where will you get the money from?

There is no eco-system for early stage capital in India. We are trying to create one in our company CARMa, wherein we are partnering with educational institutions to set up incubators which provide, amongst other things, pre-seed capital. CARMa is also in the process of setting up a unique, online early stage capital raising platform for enterprises that need capital between ₹ 25 lakhs - ₹ 5 crores.

We have identified this as our 'sweet spot' because our logic is that under ₹ 25 lakhs you have access to debt in whatever form and above ₹ 5 crores, you have access to equity. It is in this range that you have access to neither.

But at the moment, the only way you can raise capital is by approaching, what we call the 3 F's – friends, family and father-in-law! There is no other source of funding in the proto-stage. If you have a game-changing product, you may be able to attract equity funding after you have been able to offer what is commonly called 'proof of concept', which means that you have been able to showcase that there are customers who are willing to put their hands in their pockets, take their wallets out and put the money in your pocket!

In my experience with all you start-up entrepreneurs, the one thing I have found common is your ignorance when it comes to capital-raising. All of you assume that your idea is brilliant and there will be a queue of venture capitalists at your door, waiting to fund you. All of you believe, naively, that you need ₹ 50 lakhs and any VC should be able to give it to you. There seems to be some glamor quotient attached to being VC-funded.

These are some of the home-truths that I'd like to share with you about capital-raising:

1. Rarely do VCs look at anything less than $5 million. Of late, I have come across some high-impact social ventures getting funded by VCs to the tune of a million, but such instances are very few and far between.

2. It is not enough to look for external funding. You need to be ready for it. In India, most startups don't raise capital because they are not investment-ready yet. Being investment-ready means doing all the right things, in terms of product, market, value-creation, team, planning, business plan, partnerships, and vision.

3. You have both debt and equity options. Both have their upsides and down sides. In the life of any business, there is a time when debt is more appropriate and there are other times when equity funding will give you an exponential trajectory. Wisdom lies in knowing when to go for debt and when, equity. In any case, in the start-up stage, there is hardly any window for the equity option.

●   **Revenue Streams**

It is not enough to feel excited that you have a great idea. You also need to know clearly how to make money from that idea. If you are in the fast food business, for instance, you must identify all the areas from where you can make money. Let's look at some possibilities:

1) Food (served in-house)

2) Take-away (your margins are high here because customers are not using your infrastructure but are paying the same price as those who are eating in-house).

3) Home delivery (free up to a certain radius, chargeable beyond it)

4) Cross-selling (if you buy a burger, brownie will be 50% cheaper)

5) Up-selling (when a customer orders a 10-inch pizza, you say, this costs you ₹ 100 but a 16-inch pizza costs you just ₹ 120, so why don't you buy that)

6) Value selling (a soft drink is free if your purchase is more than ₹ 200)

7) Continuity selling (buy for ₹ 300 now and we will give you a discount of 10% on your next bill)

8) Loyalty (buy six times from us in three months and you will become eligible for a gold card)

9) Event-centric (we have a stand-up comedian performing today so there is a cover charge)

10) Viral (you create your own recipe and we will shave 10% off the price for all the customers who go for it and give you the money)

11) Personal touch (celebrate your kid's birthday here and we will put the pictures of the birthday bash on our bulletin board).

These are some of the ways in which with the same set of standard products, a fast food joint can create multiple revenue streams for itself.

A good business plan necessarily has to have multiple revenue streams, whether it is for a brick-and-mortar business or for an internet business. In the former, it is still easy to identify main revenue streams, but in the latter, somehow the imagination is limited to generating revenue from advertising.

I find this extremely frustrating. For one, advertising on the internet is steadily losing both its charm and edge. For another, for a start-up, the revenues accruing from advertising are not enough to prop a sustainable and scalable business model.

Let us see what the options are for an internet business to generate revenue, besides advertising. Let's say the business is an online cricket portal which aggregates information on cricket:

1) Subscription (offer a vanilla service which is free, any value-added service is for a fee, *eg.* World Cup final match details free, posters of Sachin and Dhoni for a fee)

2) Sale of merchandise and memorabilia

3) Tickets to a match

4) Event-centric (Virat Kohli is coming to our office, 20 tickets are auctioned, the three highest bidders get to have a coffee with him)

5) Online events (cricket-related quiz, scrabble etc. with an entry fee)

6) Packaged tours to cricket stadia around the world

7) Book-reading on-line with author for a fee

The possibilities are limitless. You just have to be creative and smart. You have to remember your basic Economics – Wants are unlimited but resources are limited!

- **Cash Flow**

If you have estimated your resource requirement fairly accurately and if you are on track in terms of when your sales will generate revenue, your cash flow should not really be a challenge. Each trade has its own set of practices. If you are selling directly to the end user, in most cases, it will be a cash up-front business. For instance, if you have your own high-end shoe boutique, your customers will pay you before they walk out of your store.

If you are selling to a channel, there may be a credit period. For example, if you are making masala powder and selling it to retail outlets, typically the credit period may range anywhere between 15-180 days. So it is important that you learn to factor this in your cash planning. If you plan on the basis of sale, you may not have enough money in your kitty to rotate and make payments to your service providers. So a good discipline is to plan on the basis of when your money will come into your account before deciding on pay-out dates.

● **Plan for contingencies**

Be prepared that all planning is only to make you feel good. It does not guarantee that everything will go according to your script. So make sure you build enough redundancies in your system. Given the volatility of markets today, plan B is passé. You are better off going right down to plan Z!

> **TAKEAWAYS from step 6**

1. *It is imperative to plan your resource requirement for the next one year to understand your costs and your capital requirement.*

2. *Be realistic while planning your expenses – don't underestimate.*

3. *Remember that there are simple yet effective ways to cut your costs.*

4. *Identify multiple revenue streams for your business. Don't curb your business because you lack the imagination.*

5. *Always have, not one but several back-up plans. You never know what could go wrong.*

STEP 7

HOW DO YOU WRITE YOUR BUSINESS PLAN?

"A GOAL WITHOUT A PLAN IS
JUST A WISH."

– ANTOINE DE SAINT-EXUPERY

As I see it, four questions plague all start-up entrepreneurs.

- Did Bill Gates do a business plan?

- Who should do the business plan?

- When should I do the business plan?

- And finally, what exactly *is* a business plan?

Let's answer each of them so that these questions are buried forever.

- Did Bill Gates do a business plan? Honestly I don't know. If he did, and used it to build a great company like Microsoft, good for him. It just means that doing a good business plan is a pre-cursor to building a good business.

If he didn't, well, he must be truly great because, despite not doing a business plan, he did build Microsoft. But then my next tongue-in-cheek repartee to you would be, just imagine what a better Microsoft he could have built if only he had done a business plan!

Hidden beneath this innocent question is a very loaded hypothesis. All those who do great business plans build great businesses. Conversely, those who don't, fail miserably as entrepreneurs.

Neither is true, but honestly, does it matter? Writing the business plan is a good way of reducing uncertainty in the business and mitigating risks. As it is, as an entrepreneur, your life is full of twists and turns, googlies and carom balls. Anything that will make it even a tad smoother should be embraced without debate. That's how I look at it. A business plan is a must-have because it is a good-to-have. So kill the debate and just do it.

- Who should do the business plan? I'm always amused when entrepreneurs ask me this. My reply is, when you ask a girl out on a date, do you ever ask, should I go or should I send my friend? Then why does this question come up at all as to who should do the business plan? Isn't it a foregone conclusion that the one who has envisioned the business should do the business plan?

I have known entrepreneurs paying an arm and a leg to consultants to get a fancy business plan made. They justify it by saying that they are not good at writing business plans and hence they have taken professional help.

I have always told my mentees: A good business plan is not about colorful layout and design, nor is it about complex wordplay. A good business plan should speak to you in the voice of the entrepreneur, should compel you to share his vision, and should draw you into its magic. It should dare you to challenge the unreasonableness of it all. It does not matter if it's visually appealing or if the language is not Queen's English.

All that matters is whether you have been able to communicate your passion and conviction through this document enough for people to join hands with you either as employees, or customers, or partners, or investors.

So banish this question from your mind and repeat after me. Who writes the business plan? "I do!"

- When should I do the business plan? The best time is now. Follow the steps in this book and you will arrive at the answer. This is Step 7, so do all the things that we have discussed till now and then sit down to write your business plan.

- What is a business plan? I have heard very many definitions. Some say it's a road map. Others say it's a resource-estimation document. Still others say it is all about financials. My answer is, yes it is all of it and more. It is the blueprint of your business so it has to necessarily include resource-estimation and planning and it has to have P&L and cash flow and balance sheet and all of that.

To me, a business plan is the entrepreneur's wish list.

I always tell my mentees, when you're writing the business plan, let your imagination soar. Don't be constrained by the resources you have access to. For a minute just let yourself get carried away by the thought that you have a million bucks on hand and with it, you have the freedom to transform the world during your time, not after you're long gone!

The business plan is also a good reference document. As you get involved in the everyday rigor of building the business, many important things get side-lined. It is only when you go back to the business plan that you realize your acts of omission and commission. The best thing is that the business plan gives you an opportunity to course-correct then and there, before it's too late.

Very simply put, a business plan document must answer six key questions. They are:

a) What is my business idea?

b) What is the pain point it addresses?

c) Who is my customer?

d) Who is my team?

e) How much money do I need and how will I raise it?

f) How much money will I make?

These six questions also form the core of what is popularly known as an 'elevator pitch'. The phrase is borrowed from another dream-script.

Suppose you got into the elevator in your office building on the 5th floor and pressed zero. You notice that there is another gentleman riding the elevator with you. Even as you spot him, you also notice, much to your excitement, that he is Warren Buffett.

You have exactly 30 seconds before the elevator hits ground zero. What can you tell him in those fleeting 30 seconds that will grab his imagination to such an extent that when the elevator comes to a stop, he puts his hand into his pocket, pulls out his cheque book, looks you in the eye and says: "How much should I write it for?" This is the stuff wild dreams are made of but wild dreams can be made to happen if only you're prepared for them!

But to be able to answer these six questions, you need to do thorough homework such that there are no grey areas or unaddressed concerns, that you haven't ignored some fundamental issues that could have a profound impact on your business, or that you haven't shoved under the carpet some unpleasant facts just because they don't suit you.

Let's look at all the elements of a business plan keeping in mind the elevator pitch.

Executive Summary:

A good business plan should always have a 500-word executive summary which, in a nutshell, answers all the six questions. For example, the executive summary of Apple iPod might read something like this:

"Our product is a music listening device which is small enough to carry, wherever you go, without being intrusive. Our customer is someone who loves creating his own playlist and needs music all the time in his life. Our team, like our customers, live and breathe music. Not only are we hungry for creating game-changing products, we make you, our customer, equally hungry for our products. Because our product not only changes the way you enjoy music but transforms the way you live, this is how much we have spent on it and this is how much we hope to make from it."

Got it? The executive summary should be enticing enough to make anyone pick up the plan and read it from cover to cover like it is an unputdownable crime thriller!

What is the business idea?

Your business idea is about your offering or product. For example, when Air Deccan came into the market, their product was not the flight, it was not transport from point A to point B. It was low-cost, no-frills flying. In line with the theme of low-cost, they did away with thick printed tickets (they introduced online ticketing), they stopped offering free meals on flights, and they bought smaller aircrafts so the parking charges were lower. They also used unconventional channels such as petrol pumps for ticket booking, and they did away with large crews on flights. If you asked Captain Gopinath, the promoter of Air Deccan what his offering was, he would say: "Low cost airline."

This is explained in detail in Step 13 – 'Why you should develop a 'differentiated' product?'.

What is the pain point it addresses?

It could be your own pain point or it could be someone else's. Either way, you are looking at it as an opportunity. If you are the first one to address this pain point, the biggest advantage you have is that you have an opportunity to not only create a market, but the industry itself. Air Deccan did not just create a new flight service; it created a whole industry for low cost airlines.

If there are others who have seen the same opportunity and entered the market, you can do two things. You can either compete with them in the same market place with a differentiator or you can create your own new uncontested market space. For example, the TV reality show on Sony, *Jhalak Dikhla Ja*, is no longer just a dance show competing with *Nach le* or Dance India Dance.

Although it showcases dancing, it has combined so many other elements into it that it has created a whole new genre. It has fitness (you have to be seriously fit to do those impossible lifts!); it has acting (there are themes allotted, like tragedy, romance, comic act); it has creativity (not just conventional dance styles but the choreographer is allowed to invent his/her own combinations); it has music (remixed to suit the pace, tempo and emotion of the dance sequence) and of course it has loads of drama! So it has gone way past just being a dance show and has become a wholesome entertainer.

Who is my customer?

This is the biggest challenge of them all both in building a business and in writing a business plan. Start-up entrepreneurs pay more attention to developing their product than to discovering their customer. The assumption seems to be that if you put out a good product in the market place, people will automatically flock to it. This is old-world thinking and does not work anymore because today, the customer is supremely empowered and has learnt to exercise his right of choice.

How many youngsters go to a Harley Davidson dealership and ask for a test ride before buying? Chances are that they have more thorough knowledge about the bike – its price and its performance – than anyone in the dealership. Brand loyalty is old-fashioned and people take pride in announcing to the world that they are 'brand sluts'! Go with whoever offers you a good time!

This is explained in detail in step 14, 'How do you put a face to your customer?'.

Who is my team?

During the dotcom boom, investors were enamored only by the business idea and all their bets were based on how new it was or how game-changing it was. Rarely did they give weightage to the teams that had germinated it or were backing it.

Post the dotcom bust, the founding and the management team have gained primacy in the scheme of things and investors are drawn more by the team than by the idea. So even if the idea is trail-blazing, if the team behind it demonstrates mediocrity by way of execution skills, investors are backing off. Conversely, the idea may be a 'me-too', an ordinary one, but if the team behind it consists of high performers with an established track record, investors are aligning themselves to it.

Three things work in the entrepreneur's favour when he's approaching a customer or an investor. They are: passion and track record of the founding team; competence and sense of purpose of the management team; and the robustness and credibility of the Advisory Board.

We have already talked about the founding team in Step 4. In Step 10, how and what kind of a management team you should hire has been discussed in detail. In your Advisory Board, you should have a mix of people from your domain, your industry, your corporate circle, someone who is very well-connected, your mentor, and a couple of people whom you trust. Also, keep the Advisory Board young. Don't fill your Board with retired people just because they are available or because you think their grey hair will compensate for your lack of experience!

Read Step 10 'How do you hire the right team?' to know more.

How much money do I need and how can I raise it?

The only way you can estimate how much money you need is by calculating all your costs. There are two stages to your cost calculation. The first stage is when you are developing the product and have not yet gone to market. The second is when you have begun to acquire paying customers but the revenues are not enough to meet all your expenses. In both the stages you have to identify costs correctly and judiciously so that you are able to allocate funds for it.

We have already discussed estimating costs in detail in the previous Step.

Once you have estimated the resources you require, the next question you have to answer is: "Where will I get the money from to meet my expenses?" Unfortunately no one funds the vision of the entrepreneur. All the investors will tell you: "Show me your paying customers!"

Now it's a catch 22 situation. You need to develop your product first before you get your customers. But you need money to develop your product. You may not even have enough to develop a prototype. What do you do?

There are only two options. One is to convince your college to set up incubator with a corpus for seed/pre-seed funding. The other is to raise it from the 3 F's – friends, family and father-in-law!

Step 18 illustrates the need for incubators and how they can be set up. Step 8 tells you how to raise money to fund your business.

How much money will I make?

When asked by journalists what their projection for revenues is three years from now, I have often heard many CEO's say that all they know is for a quarter and that three years is too far away to be predicted in this dynamic ever-changing world. I know where they're coming from but I find their short-term vision a little hard to digest. My boss in UTV, Ronnie Screwvalla, was very fond of saying that there is no long-term without the short-term. I agree. But I also believe that you can't be so focused on the short-term that the long-term is nowhere on your radar.

Once you have definitively identified your customer, translating that to revenues is a matter of simple arithmetic.

It is very important that you identify multiple streams of revenues in any business, as we have already seen in the previous Step.

Now let's do a business plan for a live case. Let's take the case study of the business I drive in our company CARMa, which is Capacity Building and Mentoring (CARMa Sutra) and write a business plan for it.

Executive Summary:

CARMa Capacity Building and Mentoring Services (CBMS) mentors start-ups to execute their vision from ideation to profit; mature enterprises to hit the growth trajectory with an infusion of new ideas and capital; and family business to overcome legacy mind-sets and align the best of their heritage to the current market trends. CBMS is a collaborative model and has more than 130 mentors from across the globe and from different domains in its network on a revenue-sharing basis. These mentors are either real-time entrepreneurs or senior corporate professionals who 'think' like entrepreneurs. CARMa CBMS plans to have hundred mentees in year I who will bring in a revenue of ₹ 10 million and since it is cash up front, we are not looking to raise capital in year one.

What is my business idea/product/offering?

It is capacity-building and mentoring start-ups, mature enterprises and family business to become investment-ready through an intense half-yearly program called CARMa Sutra. The program works like this: the entrepreneur is asked to identify three areas he wants to be mentored on. The reason for this is to get the entrepreneur to zero in either on his vulnerable areas or his priority areas where he needs mentoring.

These areas then become the Scope of Mentoring in the Mentorship Agreement. The scope is further broken down into milestones for two reasons: Firstly, the mentoring engagement is a milestone-driven one unlike a consulting engagement which is driven by billable hours and secondly, it becomes easy to track progress for both mentor and mentee.

One lead mentor is then assigned to the mentee. The mentor need not be a domain expert but he should necessarily be an organization-builder. He may in turn bring other mentors from time to time for specific activities.

The entire engagement costs ₹ XYZ plus service tax for the whole program.

So far we have not done any business development. Since one of our co-founders writes a regular monthly column for the magazine Entrepreneur, all our mentees have approached us on their own after reading the column.

What is the pain point?

There are several pain points in India.

We don't become entrepreneurs because we don't know how to. The reason we don't know how to, is because no one teaches us the basics of entrepreneurship in college.

We also don't become entrepreneurs because no one in our eco-system encourages us. Even if our parents are entrepreneurs, they will still discourage us by saying that we're better off taking up a good, secure job in an MNC.

In schools and colleges, systematically we are taught to do the same mindless things by rote and creativity is decimated. Becoming an entrepreneur means being creative. Since we have lost our creativity, we have lost our spirit of entrepreneurship too.

Failure in business is frowned upon and stigmatized. Since becoming an entrepreneur means high risk of failure, we shun it. We don't want our friends and neighbors pointing fingers at our family members saying that their son/daughter is a failure. So it is not just about failing in business, somehow the connotation is that we are failures as human beings too.

We have not yet learnt the value of having mentors in building successful businesses. We still think mentors are a good-to-have, not a must-have. CBMS addresses all the above pain points.

Who is my customer?

All entrepreneurs who are open to the idea of mentoring and all enterprises that are ethical and scalable are our customers. They may be start-ups, mature enterprises or family business. They may be in any domain, in any geography, at any phase of the business. CARMa CBMS is domain-and- phase agnostic. Since most of the mentoring is online, entrepreneurs can be in any part of the world. They have to be conscious that they need mentoring, they should articulate what are the areas they need mentoring on, they should be receptive to the rigor of mentoring and they should be clear with respect to the outcome of mentoring.

Who is my team?

We are three co-founders who bring very complementary skill sets to the table. Hemant is a capital raising specialist and a serial entrepreneur who has set up and run successful businesses in Kenya and Australia and is very well-networked. Vaishali is a Kidologist who specializes in conducting workshops on creativity for teens and pre-teens, their parents and teachers. Nandini has spent 20 years in the corporate sector on all inhabited continents and for the last six years has been teaching entrepreneurship and mentoring entrepreneurs. Nandini has mentored over 500 entrepreneurs absolutely free in her company Startups.

We have put together a young but experienced, passionate, vibrant team who are driven by the fact that they meet such amazing entrepreneurs from across India on a day-to-day basis and get to learn from them. Each mentee who enters our mentorship program brings with him his knowledge of the business, his ambition, his vulnerability, and his passion for not only growing the company but also for his own personal growth.

For the team, it is quick-fix, short-cut intense on-the-fly lesson in entrepreneurship!

We have also got a very competent, experienced but young, hands-on Advisory Board of people drawn from different walks of life. They bring not only mastery and purpose to the table but their network too.

CARMa CBMS is a collaborative model, so if someone is doing something in a small region or in a limited way, we partner with him, share the revenue and hit the ground running. We are not interested in re-inventing the wheel, nor are we interested in people who operate in silos.

How much money do I need and how will I raise it?

Our main expenses in Year I are infrastructure (rent, electricity, communication), payroll, travel and mentor fees. It comes to a total of ₹ 4 million.

Our revenue in Year I is ₹ 10 million. Since we take the mentoring fee up front at the time of signing the agreement, we are self-sufficient and don't need to raise capital.

How much money will I make?

We will have revenues of ₹ 10 million and a profit of ₹ 6 million in Year I. This is from mentoring alone. There are also other services that CBMS provides such as capacity-building workshops and setting up of incubators in colleges, whose revenues are not included here.

Broadly, this is what a business plan looks like. You need to keep on hand all your support documents of course, particularly your financials in terms of balance sheet, P&L, and cash flow. It is also good to do the financials for at least three years.

You also need to state all your assumptions clearly and your Plan B if those assumptions go awry.

You should also include a paragraph on what are the risks that you perceive and how you can convert them into opportunities.

You should also discuss in detail what your marketing strategy is, how do you plan to acquire your customers, what are the collaterals you have created, what is your branding strategy and how you plan to grow the business in the next couple of years, whether you would be looking for capital to take the company to the next level etc.

It would be good to include an organogram that clearly explains your organization structure.

With that, it will become a complete, well-rounded business plan.

> TAKEAWAYS from step 7

1. The business plan is the entrepreneur's wish list. Don't be bound by the availability of resources. Be unreasonable in your thinking!

2. Writing the business plan is a good way of reducing uncertainty in the business and mitigating risks.

3. YOU and only you should write the business plan. Don't burn a hole in your pocket trying to get a fancy one made by a consultant. He doesn't share your passion – it's not his business plan.

4. Your business plan MUST answer these six questions:

   a) What is my business idea?

   b) What is the pain point it addresses?

   c) Who is my customer?

   d) Who is my team?

   e) How much money do I need and how will I raise it?

   f) How much money will I make?

5. Once your business plan is ready, come hail or storm, you know exactly what to expect.

STEP 8

HOW DO YOU RAISE MONEY?

"IT'S NOT THE EMPLOYER WHO PAYS THE WAGES. EMPLOYERS ONLY HANDLE THE MONEY. IT'S THE CUSTOMER WHO PAYS WAGES."

– HENRY FORD

It is tragic that most of you spend more time obsessing about how to raise money than developing a differentiated product. It is even more tragic that this behaviour is not just from young student entrepreneurs; even older people who have over a decade's work experience under their belt display the same lack of maturity when it comes to money.

Let's look at some basics. When you want to raise money, there are two options- debt and equity.

Debt is when someone gives you the money that you need as a loan. If your father has given you the money, it may not carry any interest; if someone else in your network has given you the money, he will expect that you return the money with interest, in a mutually agreed time-frame. If bank has lent you money against collateral, there will be a fixed schedule of payment for the principal and the interest over a pre-determined time frame.

Equity is when someone gives you money against stake in your company. This could be an angel investor, typically someone who is known to you and your family or to someone in your network. Or it could be the Y Combinator model which was developed in the US in 2005 where, twice a year, they fund small amount of money (say $18K) in a large number of start-ups (anywhere between 25-50), and the start-ups are intensely mentored in the Silicon Valley over the next three months so that the entrepreneur can refine his business model and make it investor-attractive.

In India, Morpheus Ventures is attempting the Y Combinator model. This is a model that should become an integral part of any entrepreneurial habitat, because what start-ups need in the early stages is not just money but mentoring too and this model makes sure that the entrepreneurs receive the requisite mentoring from expert mentors. It works well for Y Combinator too because by providing mentoring support, they are able to mitigate the risk of high mortality of start-ups.

I am not going to discuss Venture Capital funding here for one simple reason. Remember this book is about start-ups which are getting market-ready. Until they have acquired their first several paying customers, and unless they are able to demonstrate that their business models are capital intensive (upwards of $5 million), they will not be able to attract VC's.

The biggest upside of debt is that you don't have to give up stake in your company, but the biggest downside is, you have to factor loan repayment in your monthly cash flow, especially if you have taken a bank loan.

The biggest upside of equity funding is that there is neither any interest to be repaid nor is there a monthly outflow. But the first biggest downside is you don't know what the correct valuation of your company is, and since you are desperate to raise money, you are more likely to under-sell. When your company starts earning and growing, you will regret your hasty decision.

The second biggest downside of equity funding is that in your hurry to raise money, you may bring on board people who are culturally and ideologically very different from you. So even if you have money, product, customer, and everything else going for you, this may become the show-stopper.

As far as India is concerned, there is no eco-system for early stage equity. Like I said earlier, the only two equity options are an angel investor (someone in your known network, a professional investor, or sometimes your own customer or your supplier may take a stake in your company, or a mentor), or a Y Combinator model investment company. It is too early days to attract equity investments from VC.

Let's quickly look at some of the options that are available to fund your start-up:

1. Bank loan:

This is a viable option only if you are a manufacturing company. You can do a detailed 'project report' (same as business plan, but each bank has its own format), offer land and machinery as collateral (in fact you can offer the resources that you need for your business as collateral, in which case your land and machinery will be 'hypothecated' to the lending Bank till you clear the loan. But banks only give you anywhere between 40-50% of the value of land and machinery as loan). If you have any other collateral besides the one you need for business, you can raise up to 75% as loan from the bank and the balance margin money has to be mobilized by you either from your own funds or from elsewhere.

If you are an internet business, no bank will fund you. They behave like Warren Buffett, and turn their faces away saying they don't understand technology businesses! So here, if you have any collateral, you can raise a personal loan and use it to fund the business.

Of late, SBI, Canara Bank, even SIDBI, have begun to offer un-collateralized loans from anywhere between ₹ 10 lakhs to a crore. But the time they take to process the application can be anywhere between 4-6 months and this combined with the documentation protocol may drive you up the wall.

2. Raising loan from friends and family :

This is the best way if you are lucky to have people in your ecosystem who have the money to give you. They are funding you because they trust you and they have your interest at heart. Try and sell your vision to as many people as you can. By now, you would have done the business plan and estimated your resource inflows and outflows in fair amount of detail. So rustle up a little more than what you actually need so that it can take care of all contingencies. If raising money from one source is difficult, try and raise smaller tranches from your close friends and family members. This is where it helps if you are three to four co-founders. Each one of you can tap into your network.

3. Bootstrap :

This means that you don't raise any money at all, but from day one, you are able to go to your customer and all your expenses are met with from your sales revenue. This is possible only if you are in the 'service' business where you don't need time to build a product. For example, you have taken on a canteen contract in a corporate campus where they have provided all the hardware, the customers, and the infrastructure. So all you do is deploy the given resources, cook, sell and make money.

The second scenario where bootstrapping is possible is when you are a franchisee. Suppose you are an employee of HP and you come to know that they are looking to appoint franchisees. Typically their first preference will be to someone like you who understands the market, the organization and the work culture. So they will be more than delighted to have you resign and become a franchisee. In which case, they may be lenient in terms of the up-front payment that you need to make, and they may even give you a 'soft loan' for the initial expenses of setting up the franchise business. They have in any case given you ready made products and market, so you can manage all your expenses from the sales revenue.

There have also been instances where even in the product business, entrepreneurs have managed to partner with their customers from day one, scheduled their inflows in such a way that the client pays up a portion of the total project cost up front, and the balance are linked to regular milestones. Here again, you don't need any other money to fund your expenses.

4. **Remain in employment till you're market ready:**

The best way to my mind, to fund your start-up, is to continue in job till you are ready to go to market. The way this works best is if there are multiple co-founders.If there are two of you, for instance, one of you can get involved in overseeing the team that is building the product and the other continues in a job so that there is regular cash flow to take care of some basic payroll expenses. I also know a number of young entrepreneurs who work in the day and develop the product at night, and quit the job only when the product is market-ready. If the product that you are developing is in the same domain as your job, life becomes that much easier.

5. **Foundation Grants :**

There are also grants that are available. National Innovation Foundation (NIF) and TePP, are the brain-child of Prof Anil Gupta. NIF supports innovation in the informal sector whereas TePP is a national platform that funds individual innovators across the country. The Department of Science and Technology also has grants for innovative ideas. The key thing here is that grants are made available only to those products which have patent potential.

If you are a social entrepreneur, you can also approach Aga Khan Foundation, Ford Foundation, Cherie Blair Foundation, Acumen, Kauffman Foundation, Omidyar Foundation, Bill and Melinda Gates Foundation etc., by demonstrating the high- density social impact potential of your business idea.

6. **Personal Savings :**

The biggest upside of becoming an entrepreneur after working for a decade or so in large organizations is that you are able to put aside some capital from your savings. The other biggest upside of course is the network that you will be able to build. When you are a plural founding team, it is that much more power as you can use the savings of all of you and the network.

7. **Get rid of stuff you don't need :**

A mentee of ours sold his mountaineering equipment on ebay for ₹ 500,000, because he figured, as an entrepreneur in the start-up stage, he wouldn't have much time to go mountain climbing and therefore the equipment would go waste. That money came in very handy and he made so much money over the next five years that he now buys all his climbing stuff from Patagonia, which is the world's premium outdoor equipment company!

8. **Mobilise!:**

This is a good time to remember all loans given to friends in the past, tax refunds, bonds to be redeemed, shares to be sold, privilege leave to be encashed, incentives to be collected, statutory dues to be transferred, gratuity to be mopped!

9. **Credit cards:**

Banks these days are big on selling credit cards without too much background check. It has become fashionable even for impecunious youngsters to have a wallet full of credit cards. Use them for funding your business! But make sure that you are also able to pay in time without piling up interest.

10. **College Incubator:**

This is your best bet. Convince your college to set up an incubator, create a corpus from various sources including alumni network, get yourself incubated there so you have access to mentor, pre-seed capital, infrastructure and support services.

There are ivy league educational institutions that have good business incubators. IIMA has Centre for Innovation, Incubation and Entrepreneurship which calls for business plans, the selected ones get access to an intense two week mentorship program at IIMA, mentors are assigned and the business is incubated.

IIMB has NS Raghavan Centre for Entrepreneurial Learning which offers pre-seed capital, mentorship, infrastructure and support services.

Many of the IIT's and NIT's also have technology incubators.

But typically, the college incubators are technology incubators only.

11. **Sub-let office:**

If you are lucky enough to own your office space, consider the option of letting out a portion for rent. A mentee of ours owned 1600 SFT of office space in prime location. He kept 300 SFT for himself. He let out the balance to five separate companies which fetched him a total rent of ₹ 73,000 per month. Plus, since in Bangalore there is also the system of 10 months' rent payable as deposit, he always had enough cash in the system to rotate!

12. Freelance/Moonlight:

Even if you don't want to take up a full time job, take on assignments that keep cash coming regularly.

13. Use any available real estate for advertising:

If you have office space and you can sell space for billboard/hoarding for a lucrative monthly revenue, go for it.

14. Business Plan competitions:

Don't miss them. They give you visibility, they give you opportunity to tweak your business model, they open doors for you in terms of networking and most important, when you win, they bring big bucks. The TiE mentorship programs for instance call for business plans and the winners get ₹ 25 lakhs as prize money. ISB, Hyderabad has a similar competition. Canaan Partners, Kauffman Foundation etc., all give you a head-start if you prepare adequately and win the competitions.

The Boulder, US, based Unreasonable Institute (www. unreasonable institute.org) competition gives you money, international exposure, networking opportunity with investors and access to mentors.

Like I said earlier, most of you get stuck because you only obsess about raising money form VC's. If you are smart, there a many different ways of raising money and you can do one or all of the above at different points in time to keep the cash flowing into the system.

> TAKEAWAYS from step 8

1. *Forget VC at this stage*

2. *Leverage your own network for raising seed money.*

3. *If you are smart, you can always raise money.*

4. *There are at least 14 different ways listed up here. You can use any of them or all of them at different points in time to ease your cash flow.*

STEP 9

HOW DO YOU GIVE LEGAL FORM TO YOUR BUSINESS ENTITY?

"THE ONLY TRUE LAW IS
THAT WHICH LEADS TO FREEDOM,"
JONATHAN SAID.

– JONATHAN LIVINGSTON SEAGULL

Now that you have completed your business plan, the next thing you need to do is to create a legal entity under which you can run the business.

You have several options for a legal entity. The most popular ones are:

1. Proprietorship
2. Partnership Business
3. Company
4. Limited Liability Partnership (LLP)

Let's look at each one of them to understand their advantages and disadvantages.

Proprietorship

This is essentially a one-man show. The man running the show is called a Proprietor. Go through the points listed below carefully to understand it and if it suits your business, then go for it.

- Easy to start up, it is the simplest of all.

- Very minimal regulatory approvals required (almost none).

- Capital investment is dependent upon the financial stability of proprietor.

- The business is not separate from the proprietor. The proprietorship is not a different legal entity from that of proprietor. Proprietor = Proprietorship.

- Unlimited liability – this means that if the proprietor owes money to people he has done business with and there is not enough in the business, then he will have to pay out of his personal assets.

- Risk and Return – High

- If the business makes losses, all the losses are to be borne by the proprietor only. If the business booms, and makes a lot of profit, all the profit will go to the proprietor only.

- Proprietor = Decision Maker. The buck stops with the proprietor. If he has good decision-making capabilities, his business will flourish; if he doesn't, the business will flounder.

- If the proprietor dies or if he is incapacitated in any way, the business will shut down.

- The approximate cost of starting a proprietorship business in India is ₹ 5000/-.

- Capital Investment depends entirely on the Proprietor.

Partnership business

Simply put, a partnership business is: Proprietor 1 + Proprietor2 +....... = Partnership

- Two or more members, known as partners, join hands to form an association to run the business.

- Governed by the Partnership Act, 1932.

- A formal document known as a 'Partnership deed' is prepared between partners as a Memorandum of Understanding amongst themselves. This describes the profit-sharing ratio, capital contribution, rights, liabilities and duties of each partner.

- Approval from 'Registrar of Firms' is optional.

- Advantage: Two heads better than one – Better decision-making.

- As two or more people are involved, a higher capital contribution is expected.

- Like in proprietorship, it is unlimited liability. Partners are not separate from the partnership. The partnership has no different legal entity from that of partners. Partnership can neither sue nor get sued, it's always the partners.

- Each partner is liable for the act of other partners as well as that of partnership. Like in proprietorship, the partners' personal assets will be at stake in case there is not enough money to pay its creditors.

- Risk and Return – Shared between Partners.

- Both profits and losses are shared between Partners.

- Like in proprietorship, death or any other incapacity of all partners will make the business to close down.

- Approximate cost of starting a partnership business in India is ₹ 10000/-.

- Capital Investment depends on capital contribution by each partner.

Limited Liability Partnership (LLP)

- A mix of traditional partnership with unlimited liability and corporate governance structure of the Company to encourage entrepreneurship and professionalism.

- Gives the benefits of limited liability to the partners and the flexibility to work out their internal structure in a mutually arrived at agreement. Ideally suited for early stage enterprises giving them the opportunity to be small and nimble-footed, yet attractive to early stage investors.

- The LLP is a corporate and legal entity separate from its partners.

- The LLP is formed when Partners join hands to include their names in the incorporation document and file it with the Registrar of Companies.

- The LLP remains in perpetual existence, irrespective of change of Partners.

- The Partnership Agreement between LLP and its Partners governs the rights, duties and responsibilities of the Partners and the LLP.

- The minimum number of people required to form an LLP is two and at least one of them should be a resident of India.

- Approximate cost of starting an LLP in India is ₹ 17000/-.

- Capital Investment depends on capital contribution by each partner.

Company

- Governed by The Companies Act, 1956, as amended from time to time.

- Complex regulations.

- The owners are separate from the company. Death or other incapacity of members does not render the company to close down.

- The management is different from members. Board of directors is appointed to manage the business activities. This form encourages professional management.

- Separate legal entity – a company can sue and get sued, in its own name.

- Limited liability – each member's liability is only to the extent of shares held by him.

- Transparency in business activities – vital documents of the company can be accessed by general public to assess the company's affairs.

- Ability to raise funds from general public – in case of a public company.

- Advantage: Better public image – 'Being a corporate'.

- Types of companies:

  a. Public Limited Company (not an option for a start-up)

      i.   Minimum seven members
      ii. Minimum three directors
      iii. ₹ 500000 minimum capital contribution

b. Private Limited Company

   i. Minimum two members

   ii. Minimum two directors

   iii. ₹ 100,000 minimum capital contribution

   iv. Approximate cost of starting a company in India is ₹ 25,000

● Once you have decided to go with a private limited company, the following step must be taken for incorporating one :

1. Apply for DIN (Director Identification Number)

Documents Required: Identity and Address proof and one passport size photo of the proposed directors. [Information required about directors – Name, Father's Name, Date of Birth, Nationality, Present Residential address, Permanent Residential address].

2. Apply for Digital Signature

Documents Required: Identity and address proof of the any one proposed director.

3. Apply for the availability of the name in Form 1A.

4. Select, in order of preference, at least one suitable name (up to a maximum of six names), indicative of the main objects of the company.

5. Ensure that the name does not resemble the name of any other already registered company and also does not violate the provisions of emblems and names (Prevention of Improper Use Act, 1950). You can do this by checking the availability of names on the portal itself.

6. Apply to the concerned RoC (Registrar of Companies) to ascertain the availability of name in eform 1A by logging on to the portal. The digital signature of the applicant proposing the company has to be attached in the form. If proposed name is not available, you have to apply for a fresh name on the same application.

7. After the name approval the applicant can apply for registration of the new company by filing the required forms (that is Form 1, 18 and 32) within 60 days of name approval.

8. Arrange for the drafting of the Memorandum and Articles of Association (MoA) by the lawyers, have it vetted by RoC and get 100 copies printed.

9. Arrange for stamping of the memorandum and articles with appropriate stamp duty (now online stamping facility is available).

10. Get the Memorandum and the Articles signed by at least two subscribers in his/her own hand, his/her father's name, occupation, address and the number of shares subscribed for and witnessed by at least one person.

11. Ensure that the Memorandum and Article is dated on a date after the date of stamping.

12. Login to the portal and fill the following forms and attach the mandatory documents listed in the eForm

    a) Declaration of compliance – Form-1.

    b) Notice of situation of registered office of the company – Form-18.

    c) Particulars of the Director's, Manager or Secretary – Form-32.

Submit the above eForms after attaching the digital signature; pay the requisite filing and registration fees and send the physical copy of Memorandum and Article of Association to the RoC.

After processing of the Form is complete and Corporate Identity is generated obtain Certificate of Incorporation from RoC.

Additional steps to be taken for formation of a Private Limited Company:

To obtain Commencement of Business Certificate after incorporation, the company has to make following compliance:

1. File a declaration in eForm 20 and attach the statement in lieu of the prospectus (Schedule III) or

2. File a declaration in eForm 19 and attach the prospectus (Schedule II) to it.

3. Obtain the Certificate of Commencement of Business.

   Once you have obtained the certificate, you are now legally in business!

> ## > TAKEAWAYS from step 9

1. *You must create a legal entity under which you can run the business.*

2. *It can either be a Proprietorship or a Partnership or a LLP or a Private Limited Company.*

3. *Choose the one that suits you best.*

4. *You can always change from a Proprietorship or Partnership to a private limited company any time with appropriate documentation and fees.*

5. *Private limited company is a better option as it gives 'corporate structure' to your business.*

6. *You cannot attract equity capital unless you are a private limited company.*

HOW DO YOU HIRE
THE RIGHT TEAM ?

ONE MAN MAY HIT THE MARK,
ANOTHER BLUNDER; BUT HEED NOT
THESE DISTINCTIONS.
ONLY FROM THE ALLIANCE OF THE ONE,
WORKING WITH AND THROUGH THE OTHER,
ARE GREAT THINGS BORN.

- ANTOINE DE SAINT-EXUPERY

I found an adorable picture of a McDonald team on the internet. It had four golden retrievers dressed in the McDonald menu. One had the face of a burger; the other was dressed like French fries; one wore the crown to depict Maharaja McBurger and one wore a bracelet of doughnuts. I thought this was an amazing way to illustrate that you are successful as an entrepreneur only when your team thinks, breathes, and lives your product.

I am a big fan of William Hewlett, one of the founders of HP. He had a slightly different take on hiring teams. He said: "First who, then what", meaning to say, whenever, wherever you find good people, bring them into your fold and they in turn will create a great product.

Hiring high-performance teams is a huge challenge for all start-ups. Firstly, how do you attract talent and secondly, when money is in short supply, your product is yet to be developed and it will take you at least a year to go to market and generate revenue, how do you pay your team?

How do you Attract Talent?

Somehow I feel that in a start-up, you don't manage to attract talent because you under-sell yourself. Therefore you not only get desperate but you also show your desperation. When you interview people, the first thing you tell them is that you are a start-up, as if that is a Band-Aid to hide all wounds! You offer it as an excuse and an apology!

- So why is the office so seedy? Oh we're a start-up. This is all we can afford.

- Why is there a mattress in the office? Oh we're a start-up and one of the co-founders lives here.

- Why are the salaries so much lower than market rates? Oh we're a start-up in boot-strap mode!

- Is there a job description for me? No, because we're a start-up and everyone does everything!

- Will you give me an appointment letter? No we're a start-up and haven't put such processes in place.

- Do you have a customer? No, we're a start-up. We're yet to find one!

Gee, how can an interview like this motivate anyone to join you? You didn't sound like a visionary entrepreneur, you sounded daft!

You can't explain sloppiness, inertia, bad planning, and lack of focus by saying you're a start-up and still expect people to join you. I sat through an interview a couple of years ago and came away delighted that I was not looking for a job in a start-up!

The interview went something like this. My mentee was making his first hire and he was looking for a Joomla expert. So the credentials of the candidate were established and before signing off, my mentee asked him: "Do you have any questions for me?"

Candidate (C): "Yes, a few of them. Firstly what is your product?"

Entrepreneur (E): "Oh! I can't share that with you."

C: "Fine, I understand (actually he didn't). You don't have to tell me all the details, but at least tell me what the application is, so I get an idea what your product possibly is."

E: "Sorry I will not till you come on board."

C: "How can I come on board without knowing what I'm getting into? It is like a blind date you know!" *(I liked his sense of humour!)*

E: "But that is the way it is going to be. I don't trust any of you guys. If I tell you what the product is, you will copy it in no time."

C: "If your product can be copied so easily, is it worth investing so much time and money in it?" *(A very valid point!)*

E: "Let me be the judge of that." Sulk and pout.

C: "Ok, can you at least tell me who your customer is?"

E: "Are you kidding? I haven't even developed my product yet, how can I tell you who my customer is?"

Needless to say that poor guy did not join and my mentee is still struggling to put together a team!

To my mind, hiring teams is based on a simple principle. You should hire people who get excited by your vision, who spend sleepless nights, like you, trying to crack the code, who air-thump the first customer acquisition with as much gusto as you do, and who have bought into your script – lock, stock and barrel.

A mentee of mine hired a graphic designer a couple of years ago and he had an interesting story to tell. Apparently his girlfriend insisted he choose IBM over the start-up that he had joined and no amount of convincing her on how much he loved his job helped. Finally she told him to choose between her and his job. He did. He's now a co-founder in that start-up!

How can I pay him?

Since you don't have money to pay salaries, you generously promise equity to your team. This is the biggest blunder that you can make. Equity is your hard earned sweat and blood and therefore it is expensive. Why would you want to fritter it away to your employees even before they have contributed to the growth of your company?

Very often entrepreneurs come to me asking: "How much equity should I promise my team?" It leaves me horrified. It is far cheaper to borrow from your neighborhood money-lender and pay salaries than promise equity. Equity has to be earned by the team by demonstrating its staying power even in the face of adversity; by its commitment to your vision; and by its performance, which leads to growth. So really the right time to reward your employees for all of the above is after three years. Most certainly not when you hire them.

Let's face it: You can't build a great organization without building a great team. You can't build a great team without rewarding them. There are some who look for long-term rewards while there are others who have to be rewarded in the short-term too. It is not that they are bad people or greedy people. It's just that their personal circumstances may not allow them to work for you without a salary, however much they want to, however much they are excited by your vision. So it is prudent on the part of the entrepreneur to pool in some seed money from his family and friends so that he can hire good teams that can develop the product and go to market. There are several myths in team-hiring.

a) "I will hire interns only so that I don't have to pay them!"

Partly true. But their delivery pre-supposes firstly, that they are competent, secondly, that they are committed, and thirdly, that they can work without supervision. More often than not, you have to choose between managing interns and managing your company!

b) "Since I don't have an office, everyone will have to work out of their homes."

In the entrepreneur's head, this is a huge plus. In actuality, it never works. There are very few people who can work out of homes, on their own steam, in an unstructured environment. Most people need the discipline of an office space, the interaction with peers and bosses, and a dividing line between personal and work time. There is an energy the office generates that people feed on which is crucial to the start-up.

"Since I don't have money I will get people in jobs to moonlight for me."

The biggest casualty here is accountability. Firstly, you are not paying them and so there is no reason for them to keep delivery promises. Secondly, they have told you that they are in a job and so your work is very low on priority. Thirdly, they may be passionate about your idea but making it work is not their mandate at all. I have seen so many mentees struggle with this for months on end and the conversation breaks down with both parties feeling bitter.

"We're friends so we can work together."

Not necessarily. We have seen in Step 4 how this is not true of co-founders. It's the same here. Being good friends does not mean you will be good colleagues. In fact you both have to contend with the fact that whilst you were both friends, one of you now is the boss!

"I will hire those who come cheap!"

Short-sighted idea. They will neither grow nor let you grow, and if you do manage to grow, in spite of them, sooner than later, they will become a show-stopper. So after all the time, money and effort you invested in them, you have no option but to let them go.

"Paying big bucks does not mean I get the best!"

You're absolutely right. Money can't buy talent. But your vision can. So when you're hiring people, it's critical to ask: "Why do you want to join my company?" If the answer is, "I'm enthralled by your vision", then follow it up with other related questions to make sure he's not saying it because he thinks that's what you want to hear. If he says because your office is close to where he lives, send him on his way! If he says he wants to join because it is only in a start-up that he can learn so many things in the shortest possible time, hire him. He's hungry for learning and he'll make your customers hungry for your products.

"I will hire people who think like me!"

When you say, 'think like me', if you mean people who share your values, your optimism, your vision, then you're absolutely right. You should hire them.

But if you mean that you will hire only those people who say 'yes' to everything that you say, then you're heading for trouble. I always tell my mentees, take stock of what you're good at, and what you're not good at, before hiring people. Then find people who are good at what you're bad at. That's the only way you will build a team with enviable, complementary skill-sets.

As entrepreneurs, you are notoriously insecure people and the typical tendency is to hire someone who's less competent than you are because that way, you will never feel threatened. But a strategy like this is bad for business and it is very important to build a team with 'different thinking' people so that oxygen is in circulation and you don't end up as dead fish!

> TAKEAWAYS from step 10

1. *The measure of you as an entrepreneur is when your team thinks, breathes and lives your product.*

2. *Don't be apologetic that you are a start-up and never use that as an excuse for your shabbiness.*

3. *Don't offer your team stake in your company at the outset simply because you cannot pay their salaries. Equity has to be earned.*

4. *Identify your strengths and weaknesses (objectively). And put together a team with complementary skills. This will make sure you feed off each other's strengths and it will only help you build that great enterprise.*

STEP 11

HOW DO YOU CHOOSE THE APPROPRIATE TECHNOLOGY?

"IT HAS BECOME APPALLINGLY
OBVIOUS THAT OUR TECHNOLOGY HAS
EXCEEDED OUR HUMANITY."

- ALBERT EINSTEIN

Technology is a broad term and is understood differently by different people. To most people, technology is synonymous with computers and internet. But machines that improve productivity on the shop floor or produce packaging (to ensure Lays chips do not become soggy) are also technology. The discussion in this chapter however is restricted only to internet technologies.

I have broadly divided entrepreneurs in to two categories for convenience. One is your typical internet entrepreneur who is creating either a web portal or aggregating buyers and sellers online or leveraging information for a particular industry. I have called this category 'internet entrepreneurs'.

The second category is any new business owner with business in any domain. It could be a manufacturing outfit, it could be a HR consultancy, it could be a newspaper, it could be a media production house or it could be a waste management company. I have called this category 'business owners'.

Let us now look at what their internet technology needs are and how they can address them.

Internet entrepreneurs

1. Data storage requirements

How much data will the website/service generate over time? This includes the number of files you would need to store online. For example, documents and simple web pages don't require much storage, but media files like audio and video will require significantly more (about 100 times more in some cases). Also, if you enable your users to upload files, storage requirements could significantly increase. Accrued over time, the more files that get uploaded, the greater will be your website's storage requirements.

Based on this information, you would want to go in for a web hosting plan that offers you plenty of storage space (many hosting providers now offer unlimited storage as part of their packages – good to consider this to help alleviate any bottlenecks down the line).

2. Traffic bandwidth requirements

How many visitors do you expect on the website? 10 a day? 100 a day? 1000 a day? This depends on who the target audience of your website is – if they are end users, you'd likely see a lot of traffic to your website over time, but if your website is targeted to a specific audience (business users, specific verticals), the visitors to your site might be lesser.

Based on this information, select a hosting plan that offers the appropriate amount of 'site bandwidth'. This is the amount of data that is transferred to and from your website. Some plans have caps on this bandwidth (10GB or maybe 50GB per month – similar to the caps that some broadband service providers have with their plans). These days, web hosting companies have plans that offer unlimited bandwidth – much more suitable for sustaining your website's growth.

3. Online transactions

Do you plan to sell services and products directly from your website? If you do, you're going to have to tie up with a payment gateway that provides access to payment services, including access to online banking systems, so people can pay using online bank transfers or credit card transactions. Some of these companies include www.ccavenue.com, www.indiapay.com, www.ebs.in. To start with, you can also sign up for services like www.paypal.com to receive funds on your websites. Also, make sure you check with your chartered accountant about the various norms, procedures and tax implications of making online transactions. To support secure transactions on your website, you will need to have secure protocols (SSL and HTTPS) enabled on your website. Make sure these capabilities are part of your web hosting plan – sometimes these need to be explicitly selected while formulating your plan.

4. Special programming expertise

At a very basic level, your website production team will need to have web programmers and web designers. The specific skills these team members would need to have depends on what you plan to implement on your website. If your site uses Flash components, special AJAX features, HTML5, formatting for mobile consumption and intensive database storage etc., you will need to hire people with these specific skills, or at least plan to bring them on board at the appropriate time.

Regarding web hosting plans, make sure you read the fine print and any asterisks you might encounter during the sign up process – web hosting providers often have inviting service plans with many goodies thrown in to start, but these are free only for the first few months after which they bill you for them. And since your web hosting payments are recurring, any wrongly selected plan could burn you with unnecessarily high on-going payments. Check their terms of service especially for opting into and out of specific web hosting features – you should be able to tailor your web hosting plans according to your changing needs, without being tied into a restrictive set of services.

Business Owners

As a new business owner, you would need to consider the key functions in the business. For example:

1. Promoting a service/product

2. Storing business data

3. How many employees, and what their functions will be

4. Determining whether employees would need regular mobile access to company data

Next, you'll need to map these requirements to technologies that will eventually fulfill the various business needs:

1. Promoting the service/product

    ● You might want to set up a website. You'll primarily need to do three things:

        i) Book the web address (called the URL)

ii)   Choose a hosting provider (the service that hosts your website and its various pages)

iii)   Build the actual website (you can do this on your own if you're so inclined, or can hire a web designer).

Note that all of these steps need recurring payments (at least yearly, depending on the plan chosen). See the links at the end for more detailed information on these three aspects.

- Using social media

  These days it is easier than ever to promote your business – use services like social networking sites such as Facebook, Twitter, and YouTube; a blogging service (Blogger, Wordpress etc.) to describe your business and propagate it. The key is keeping these communication lines always lit – try to post daily updates on what's happening in your business and keep interest in it alive. Also, you can now cross-link these channels – use tools that enable Twitter updates to appear on your blog, or blog posts to appear on your Facebook wall etc. We live in a highly-connected and cross-linked world, so make the most of it!

2. Storing/sharing business data

  - Local storage

    This is the storage on your computer/laptop. Depending on your business, you might want to upgrade the hard disk – these days you can buy a 1 Terabyte hard disk for about ₹ 3,000.

  - Attached storage

  - USB hard disks are immensely useful for porting large amounts of data between computers. Consider these devices from brands like Seagate and Western Digital – they are available from 250GB all the way to 1 Terabyte (1000GB!), and cost anywhere from ₹ 2,000 to ₹ 4,500.

- Network storage

  These devices – called Network Attached Storage (NAS) – are basically a bunch of hard disks in box that plugs directly into your office network. This enables connected users to simultaneously access work files, much like they would access a server on the network. But since this box is powered independently (and uses less power than a server,) you save on electricity and free up your actual server for other tasks.

- Cloud storage

  An interesting concept that's catching on these days – you can use one of numerous services that are based completely online. They're referred to as 'Cloud services', and they offer everything from file storage / sharing, to collaborative documents, to application hosting. Check out skydrive.live.com or documents.google.com – both of these are free services offering file storage and document collaboration respectively. Also check out YouSendIt (www.yousendit.com), a free service that provides a great way to send large files to people. Remember – because cloud services are online, you'll need to have a solid internet access provider, and one that preferably offers an all-you-can-eat access plan. Otherwise you'd possibly be overspending because of the heavy internet usage these cloud services demand.

3. Selecting hardware according to number of employees and their functions

   - Consider how many people you currently have working for you, and how big your team will eventually scale to. You'd probably need a mix of desktop and laptop computers depending on job functions. Depending on business functions, select a computer with the following key specifications:

i) Processor: Intel Core i3 (choose Core i5 or i7 for more demanding applications like graphics designing etc.)

ii) RAM: 2GB (4GB for more demanding applications)

iii) Hard disk: 500GB (1TB or more for demanding applications)

- Remember to always go in for genuine applications – these days all software updates are online, and you'll only be able to receive these updates (many of them security-related,) if you use genuine software.

- I suggest using Windows 7 as the operating system – choose your flavor (Home, Professional, Ultimate) according to your budget and requirement. Visit this link for a feature comparison of these versions: http://windows.microsoft.com/en-IN/windows7/products/compare

- You'll need solid and reliable internet connectivity to ensure business continuity. To start, a reliable 2 or 4 Mbps DSL line should suffice, but you should consider a leased line subsequently as your business grows – they provide greater reliability and better service.

4. Determining whether you and your employees would need regular mobile access to company data

- One of the biggest advantages business owners can provide to their employees is immediate, anytime access to important business data. Consider going in for one or more wireless data devices (from the likes of Reliance, Tata Photon+, Tata Docomo etc.) to deliver internet connectivity to employees on the road.

For more information on the technologies/processes mentioned in this step, visit this blog written by a mentee of ours, Marco. Here he talks about what all to consider before setting up your own website.

http://marcodsouza.blogspot.com/2008/12/setting-up-your-own-web-site-part-one.html http://marcodsouza.blogspot.com/2008/12/setting-up-your-own-web-site-part-two.html Also check out Marco's experience with using Kompozer (a free web design tool) to build your first website: http://marcodsouza.blogspot.com/2009/01/building-web-site-using-kompozer.html. To use Facebook to market your business, visit: http://www.insidefacebook.com/

The important thing is to choose the right technology for the right reason. Remember it should be an enabler, not an albatross around your neck.

> **TAKEAWAYS from step 11**

1. *Internet technologies are a must – irrespective of whether you are an internet entrepreneur or not.*

2. *Don't be afraid of using technology. If used correctly, technology can be your best friend.*

3. *If you don't know enough, turn to your mentor. Either he can directly educate you on the best available technology and how to use it, or else, put you in touch with the right people.*

4. *Choose technology that will help you cut costs and improve productivity and efficiency.*

HOW DO YOU PROTECT YOUR INTELLECTUAL PROPERTY?

"GOOD PEOPLE DO NOT NEED
LAWS TO TELL THEM TO ACT
RESPONSIBLY, WHILE BAD PEOPLE
WILL FIND A WAY AROUND THE LAWS."

- PLATO

This is not only your right but your duty as well. We have a mentee who has developed more than 25 brilliant products in the last 25 odd years and does not have a single patent. He's highly educated, lives in a metro, moves in elite circles, and yet he says it never occurred to him to protect his intellectual property. Now, he wants to sell the company but in the absence of Intellectual Property (IP), he cannot get the valuation he deserves. So we have advised him to first file for patent and then sell the company at market valuation.

IP is critical not only because you don't want someone to steal your idea and therefore your market but also because it lends robustness to your company. There are investors who will invest only in IP-protected companies. Also, IP is what differentiates your company from the rest of the players. And of course, IP can be your best entry barrier.

I have heard from young penniless entrepreneurs that they haven't filed for patent because filing costs a lot of money. Yes, it does. But not filing is a 100-times more expensive. So beg, borrow, steal or do it all – raise money and protect your IP.

IP refers to all creations of mind and intellect. It may be design for a shoe, an ice bucket, a deodorant pack, a three wheel car, a bamboo bicycle, or a portable egg holder. It may be poems, articles, essays, books, movies, painting, music, and *symbols that are used for business purposes.*

It means that if I write a poem and keep it hidden in my desk, it needs no protection. But the moment I sell it to a magazine for publication, my IP has to be protected.

Different IP rights vary in the protection they provide. Broadly, according to the *TRIPS Agreement (this is an international agreement administered by the World Trade Organization to cover different aspects of IP),* the intellectual property has been classified into:

a) *Industrial property,* which includes patents for inventions, trademarks, industrial designs, and geographic indications of source (also known as GI, which refers to certain country specific attributes. Eg, Made in

Japan or Made in Germany carry positive images of quality, precision and engineering excellence) or

b) *Copyright,* which includes literary and artistic works such as novels, poems, plays, films and musical works and the like and is now extended to include software.

What is a patent?

If you have invented a facsimile machine that stores all the faxes received and sent, you file for a patent for it. The reason you file for a patent is so that for a period of time, you can own and use it exclusively. The Government gives you that right and in giving it to you, it excludes all others from both owning it and using it commercially.

Inventions are the backbone of all innovation. Since inventions contribute to development of civilization and mankind, it is very important that the inventor is protected from others who knowingly or unknowingly may copy it and use it for their commercial success. Inventions promote not only technology but also their transfer and dissemination for public good and a patent is the best way of protecting it.

Once a patent is granted in your name, you are literally sitting on a gold mine. The patent may be in your own name or in the name of the company. If it is in the name of your company, it adds tremendously to the valuation of the company.

You can file for patent in one country or in several countries. However, patent obtained in one country is not valid in other countries. Therefore, for it to be valid, you have to file in all the relevant countries where you plan to use it for business purposes.

Administration of Patent

The metros in India – Kolkata, Mumbai, Chennai and Delhi – have patent offices to deal with the applications for patents originating within their respective jurisdictions.

There is also a Patent Information System (PIS) office located at Nagpur that maintains a comprehensive collection of patent specifications and patent related literature, on a worldwide basis. It provides technological information contained in patent or patent related literature through search services and patent document supply services.

Who can file for patent?

The inventor himself may make an application, either alone or jointly with a partner. If the inventor is dead, his legal heir may file on his behalf.

Documents required for filing an application

a) Application form in duplicate (Form 1).

b) Provisional (if your invention is still in the development stage) or complete specification (if your invention is ready for the market) in duplicate. If the provisional specification is filed, it must be followed by the complete specification within 12 months(Form 2).

c) Drawing in duplicate (if there is one).

d) Abstract Summary of the invention in duplicate.

e) Information and undertaking listing the number, filing date & current status of each foreign patent application in duplicate (Form 3).

f) Priority document (if priority date is claimed) in convention application, when directed by the Controller.

g) Declaration of inventor-ship where provisional specification is followed by complete specification or in case of convention/PCT national phase application (Form 5).

h) Power of attorney (if filed through Patent Agent).

i) Fee (to be paid in cash/check/demand draft).

Request for permission to file abroad

If you want to file for patent in another country and not in India, you need to take permission in writing from the Controller of Patents. You have to ask for permission on Form-25, along with a brief description of your invention.

Things you should be careful about

The patent is granted on a 'first to file' basis. That is, in the event there are several applications for the same invention by different people, the one who filed it first will be given the patent.

Many inventors, either because they are ignorant of patent laws and procedures or because they are over-confident, do not file for patents in time. I have even known a few entrepreneurs who either publish papers on their inventions or do a demo in international conferences even before filing for patent. In many instances, this may itself be sufficient grounds for the patent office to reject the application.

The other valid ground for rejecting the patent application is if the inventor has already commercialized the invention and then files for patent. The idea of filing the patent application is to protect its ownership before sharing it with the world. You may do so privately or confidentially if you want to validate your invention to a group of people whom you know and trust, but definitely not to the general public.

I even met an entrepreneur last year who had put his entire invention on LinkedIn! He proudly showed it to me when he approached me for mentoring. Even before I had any conversation with him, I made him take it off LinkedIn and file for patent. Happily and somewhat fortunately, he still has the patent in his name.

You also don't have to wait till your invention is fully ready. If you have an idea and a design just go ahead and file for provisional patent. You have 12 months' time thereafter to tweak your invention and file for the final one.

Just because you filed for provisional patent does not mean that you have to complete the invention. Suppose mid-way you come up with a better design, drop this and file for the new one. It is not binding on you that you have to convert the provisional application to final application if you don't want to.

What is a patentable invention?

Any new product or process which is inventive and can be used in industry is patentable. It should be new (should not exist in a similar form anywhere in India), it should not be frivolous and obvious to the expert in that area, and it should be useful in its industry.

What is not patentable?

Typically the following are described as non-patentable:

- An invention which is frivolous or which claims anything obviously contrar to well established natural laws. A balloon which sings when you burst it is a good example of frivolity. An invention which says that a man can be made into a monkey is contrary to natural laws.

- An invention which is dangerous to nature and society. (a new material for nuclear explosion)

- Something that you 'discovered' already exists in nature, for example a new type of flower or a new breed of fish or a white hole in the universe.

- Something that you 'discovered' exists in a known substance but your discovery does not really add value to the substance. For example, you may discover that the color in the red chilly is caused by a particular chemical, but your discovery does not make the chilly more valuable. Your discovery was just a result of idle curiosity.

- A cocktail that you produce by mixing two or more existing products.

- Just rearranging in a different way what already exists, for example, in a car, switching the light controls and the wiper controls from one side to the other of the steering wheel.

- A new method of growing crops or flowers.

- A new way to treat disease.

- New ways in plant-breeding.

- A mathematical or business method or a computer program per se or algorithms.

- A literary, dramatic, musical or artistic work or any other aesthetic creation including cinematographic works and television productions.

- A mere scheme or rule or method of performing mental act or method of playing game.

- A different way of presenting information.

- Topography of integrated circuits

- An invention which in effect, is traditional knowledge or which is an aggregation or duplication of known properties of traditionally known component or components.

- Inventions relating to atomic energy and the inventions prejudicial to the interest of security of India.

Publication and examination of patent applications

a)   Examination

The applications will be examined by the patent office according to serial number. If the office has any objections, it will be communicated to the applicant. If the applicant does not respond to them within 12 months of filing, the application will be abandoned.

If all the requirements are met, the patent is granted, after 6 months from the date of publication. The patent letter is then issued, entry is made in the register of patents and it is notified in the Patent Office, Journal.

b)   Publication

Once you have filed your application for patent, if you have complied with all the conditions, it will be published in the Patent Office Journal just after 18 months of filing the application. It will include date of filing, application number, name and address of the applicant. Not until it is published will it be open to public for inspection.

Term and date of patent

The term of every patent will be 20 years from the date of filing of patent application, irrespective of whether it is filed with provisional or complete specification. The date of patent is the date on which the application for patent is filed.

All these are important legal, procedural issues all of you should know about. It is good to retain a patent lawyer who can guide you through the whole filing process correctly. The filing is now possible online and the site for it is IP India Online. The screens take you through the process step by step. Don't take this lightly. Filing for patent is as important as starting your company.

> **TAKEAWAYS from step 12**

1.   *Protecting your intellectual property is not just a right but a duty.*

2.   *There is no sense in coming up with a brilliant idea and not filing for patent. Sooner than later, someone will steal your idea.*

3.   *Never talk about your invention in a public forum full of strangers without filing for patent. This can be grounds for rejecting your patent application or someone else can copy your invention.*

4.   *Focus on your business but get yourself a patent lawyer who can help you with the whole filing process.*

STEP 13

WHY SHOULD YOU DEVELOP A 'DIFFERENTIATED' PRODUCT?

"I'VE LEARNED THAT PEOPLE
WILL FORGET WHAT YOU SAID,
PEOPLE WILL FORGET WHAT YOU DID,
BUT PEOPLE WILL NEVER FORGET
HOW YOU MADE THEM FEEL."

- MAYA ANGELOU

It is mission critical that you do two things. Firstly, you identify clearly what your product or offering is and secondly, you articulate, equally clearly, what is the differentiator or value proposition in your product.

What is your offering?

Are you selling groceries or are you selling an online portal that sells groceries? Are you selling a book or are you selling a dial-a-book service? Are you selling a restaurant or are you selling information about restaurants? Are you selling your album or are you selling alternative rock? Are you selling Goa beaches or are you selling a holiday experience? Are you selling a condom or are you selling excitement?

This is not as easy as it looks. I have seen any number of business plans where this clarity is missing. It is very important that you articulate this clearly and correctly.

Many entrepreneurs get into a tizzy about whether they are offering a product or service. In today's day and age, this distinction does not matter. It is the entrepreneur's job to design the most beautiful customer experience. For example, do you go to MTR in Bangalore for the taste of the *dosa* or for the experience of eating the *dosa*, which is served on a silver platter (literally), with dollops of butter? Never mind that you have to wait in queues till your name is yelled out – it only adds to this iconic experience!

Sometimes it may be easy to say that customer experience design is through a product or a service, at other times, it may be hard, as the lines blur. For example, Bajaj two-wheelers and Maruti Suzuki cars are sought after by customers as much for their proliferating service network as for their products.

Customer experience design is an engaging, exciting and rewarding exercise. Take, for example, a customer who is interested in choosing a mobile telephony service provider. He approaches all of them to understand what each one has to offer. At this stage it is only a **conversation for possibility**. When he finally signs up with Airtel, it is not only because he likes the product but because he is impressed by so many

other things too. For instance, easy access to Airtel outlets, the courteous way the sales girl spoke to him, the confidence with which she answered all his questions, the trouble she took in recommending the right tariff-plan based on his need – all these have come together to make it a delightful customer experience that culminates in a **conversation for action.** This is the entrepreneur's first unforgettable wow moment!

Customer experience design is all about seducing the customer so that he not only comes to you, but also stays with you, is besotted by you and tells the whole world about you! He becomes your most evangelical marketer.

What value does your differentiator offer your customers?

This is as important as the offering itself. The pain point which created an opportunity for you may be individual-oriented or community-directed. For example, www.redbus.in addresses the need of an individual by offering a convenient, online, inter-state bus booking facility. A Metro transport in New Delhi, on the other hand, is meant to address the need of all Delhi-ites who need a fast, convenient transport to commute within the city.

When you are addressing a pain point, there are two likely scenarios in front of you. One is that there are other players in the market operating pretty much in the same space as you. The other is that you are the prime mover. Either way, you need a clear value proposition.

Let's see why.

If you're one of the many players in the market, you need to offer a compelling differentiator to your customer. It should be such an obvious one that not being your customer is not an option at all. Look at Bingo for example.

In a fragmented, over-crowded snack food market, they were different right from the way they entered the market. Unlike Lays, which launched different flavors staggered over time, Bingo launched a number of flavors at the same time, in one shot. This was an amazing differentiator because what it did was create phenomenal shelf-visibility. If you walked into a supermarket and went past the snack shelf, wherever you looked, you only saw Bingo. So even if you had no intention of buying any snack, you couldn't possibly ignore the attraction of so many assorted packs.

If you are the prime mover, you still have to offer a value proposition, although for a different reason. It is not to take away customers from your competitors and make them yours but to make them yours from day one so that tomorrow even if other players enter the market, they will continue to stay with you and not be tempted to move over to the other side. Look at www.cricinfo.com, which was bought by ESPN in 2007.

The company started in 1993 when there were no cricket portals and sports-related content was not accessible online. Over the last two decades, several similar sites have cropped up but www.cricinfo.com has

managed to retain such evangelical customers that no one else has ever been a serious contender to the number 1 position.

The differentiator can be in anything, ranging from product to price.

In product, it could be like the portable shower, which you carry with you, hang anywhere you like – open the nozzle and have a comfortable shower.

It could be in features like the neck-and-shoulder Moov.

It could be in price like for McDonald's when it first came to India. The very first outlet in Vasant Vihar offered burgers at ₹ 12. The logic was very simple. Market research told McDonald that on an average, every Delhi-ite spent ₹ 12 on *chaat*. So they priced their burgers in comparison with *chaat*, which was the most popular light eat in Delhi.

It could be in packaging – just remember how Tetrapak has revolutionized the juice market.

It could be in delivery. www.fashionandyou.com is a good example of this. Whilst on most internet portals you have to pay upfront through credit card for making online purchases, Fashion and You gives the customer the option of paying cash on delivery. This has brought to them customers who either did not own credit cards or who were reluctant to shop online because it meant using credit cards.

It could even be in brand communication. Again Airtel is an excellent example. In their tagline 'express yourself' was a subtle yet profound knowledge that Indians love to talk and Airtel artfully used it to say that Airtel loves to have incessantly talking customers!

The differentiator could also be in story-telling. The Economist's posters are legendary. So were ACTIONAID's advertisements that were a call-for-action in the wake of the cyclone in Orissa.

It could be in market strategy. CavinKare's Ruchi pickles for instance are hugely popular in Tamil Nadu. Soon after the launch, CavinKare realized that although pickles are a must-have in every meal, not many could afford Ruchi, which was higher priced. So they quickly launched Chinni's pickles, which were priced lower, packaged differently and was meant for customers who loved pickles but were price sensitive. The masterstroke, of course, was when they launched Chinni's pickles in 50-paise sachets so that the woman of the house could conveniently add spice to her husband's lunch box!

Value propositions are what make your business tick. And set your cash register ringing!

> **TAKEAWAYS from step 13**

1. *Identify your product's value proposition even before you have entered the market. That alone can be your strong sales pitch.*

2. *You need a value differentiator, whether you are the prime mover in the market or one of the many players.*

3. *Value differentiators not only help you acquire new customers, but also help retain your existing customers even though there are other players in the market.*

4. *Value propositions are the biggest entry barriers in business.*

5. *Top-of-the-mind recall will only come from a clear differentiator. Identify it and more importantly, articulate it.*

STEP 14

HOW DO YOU PUT A FACE TO YOUR CUSTOMER?

"WE CHOOSE OUR NEXT WORLD THROUGH
WHAT WE LEARN IN THIS ONE.
LEARN NOTHING, AND THE NEXT IS THE
SAME AS THIS ONE, ALL THE SAME LIMITATIONS
AND LEAD WEIGHTS TO OVERCOME."

— JONATHAN LIVINGSTON SEAGULL

This is the biggest challenge of them all – both in writing the business plan and building the business. If you get this right, you have yourself a winner. If you goof up on this, your business will be a non-starter.

You ask someone who is manufacturing a pencil: "Who is your customer?" and the standard answer is: "Everybody!" Why? "Because everybody uses pencil!" Everybody means who? 6.9 billion of the world's population?

Let's take an example. Suppose you have set up an upmarket, fine dining, specialty Thai restaurant in a cosmopolitan, elite area like Koramangala, Bangalore. Who are your customers? Let's look at possible options.

- Those who love Thai food and will, therefore, try out your place. If they like it, they will become your regular customers.

- Those who don't particularly like Thai food, but like trying out anything new, so they will give your place a shot once. If they like the experience, they will become your regular customers.

- Those who love Thai food to such an extent that they are extremely critical of what is currently offered in the market. They are sceptical about the new kid on the block and they come to your place just so they can shred you to pieces. But if you have a surprise in store for them, they will become your most evangelical customers.

- Those who have no cuisine preference but love fine dining. If your place offers a fine dining experience, they will become your regular customers.

- Those who don't know what Thai cuisine is and have not had too many opportunities in the past to discover whether they like it or not. Now that an opportunity has come their way, they are willing to experiment.

- Those who have members from any of the above groups in their circle/network.

- We have now established that all of these six groups have the potential to become your customer. Let's also establish who is not your customer.

- Those who are allergic to key ingredients used in Thai food, such as peanuts, tofu, coconut.

- Those who never eat out, either for health reasons or lifestyle reasons.

- Those who steer clear of Thai cuisine either because of a bad experience in the past or because of unpleasant memories associated with Thai food/Thai restaurants (*for example: a long relationship ended while at a Thai restaurant*).

- Those who think there is not much difference between Thai and Kerala cuisine, since both use coconut as their base.

- Those who don't like the vegetables – particularly the gourd family – that forms the staple in vegetarian Thai cooking.

- Those who don't like the typical smell associated with South East Asian cooking.

- Those who feel intimidated by the unfamiliar names on the menu.

- Those who think Thai is the same as Chinese. So they'd rather stick with what they are familiar with, which is Gobi Manchurian with Schezwan fried rice.

This segmentation falls under, what in Market Research is known as Psychographics or in layman terms, behaviour based on lifestyle and choices.

Now that you have a fair understanding of both who your customer is and who isn't, let's try putting a face to him. This classification in Market Research is known as demographics, or in layman terms, identifying your customer by way of age, gender, education, rural/urban, occupation, income etc.

Let's go back to your product for a minute. It is an upmarket, fine dining, specialty Thai restaurant in Bangalore in an upscale area like Koramangala.

- Let's start with age. Because it is up-market, it will never be a regular 'hangout' for college students. Hence the age group has to be 25 upwards.

- Your product is gender-neutral, in the sense that it is not like sanitary napkin which is meant only for women or a shaving cream which is meant primarily for men. So your customers will include men and women.

- It goes without saying that since you are located in Bangalore, in Koramangala, your customers are city slickers.

- Since it is a premium specialty restaurant, it is natural to expect that they will be educated and, perhaps, reasonably well-travelled since they seem to be aware of Thai cuisine.

- It is also reasonable to expect that if they are well - travelled, they are corporate professionals (especially IT), service professionals such as lawyers, doctors, etc., media and advertising professionals, successful entrepreneurs, bankers, expatriates, Indians who have come back to India after a long stint outside, or spouses of people belonging to any of the above categories.

- Naturally then, people who come here should have an income that supports an average spend of ₹ 3000-4000 per meal, for two.

- They may come to your restaurant with business partners, family members or friends.

So based on the above psychographics and demographics, your typical customer is:

Male/female, 25-55 years old, living in Bangalore city, English-medium educated with an engineering/legal/medical graduate degree or post-graduate degree in management/media/advertising, used to traveling abroad for study/work/ leisure, working professionals who may have lived and worked outside of India and finally, who have high disposable income and are not afraid to spend it on pleasure, with business partners, family and friends.

In Market Research parlance, they are bracketed as SEC-A/M,F/25-55/urban/ upwardly mobile/working professionals/ ₹ 6 lakhs + annual income/brand conscious.

Voila! You have now put a face to your customer! All you have to do is keep delighting him with a never-before-never-expected experience and he will not only bring himself to your restaurant but also Scorpio-loads of others too!

In India, customer discovery is a very layered and complex process. I have noticed that start-up entrepreneurs do not spend adequate time on this.

MNC's like Procter and Gamble have developed it into a fine art. For example, P&G brand managers are known to make cardboard cut-outs of their customers and have them in their midst during brand discussions. Suppose the product under discussion is shampoo and the brand is Pantene. They may have a cardboard cut-out of a woman called Joan who represents the typical Pantene customer. They treat Joan as if she is real and sometimes even address questions to her!

It is very important for the entrepreneur to establish this connect in order to develop a loyal and long-lasting equation with the customer.

> **> TAKEAWAYS from step 14**
>
> 1. *Not knowing who your customer means not knowing what your business is!*
> 2. *Customer discovery is not a lottery. It is a scientific process.*
> 3. *Not only know who your customer is, but also get to know him inside out!*

STEP 15

WHAT DO YOU NEED TO DO
BEFORE GOING-TO-MARKET?

HEAVEN IS NOT A PLACE,
AND IT IS NOT A TIME. HEAVEN
IS BEING PERFECT."

- JONATHAN LIVINGSTON SEAGULL

In the previous two Steps, we have seen how to develop your product and how to put a face to your customer. Now let's see what you need to do to 'take' your product to your customer.

What is marketing? When I ask this question in class, students either give me text book definitions (straight out of Philip Kotler) or they go all over the place telling me how marketing is different from selling.

Let's move away from jargon and talk commonsens. What is that one thing you absolutely need before acquiring your customer? You need a value proposition. In step 13, we saw the need for creating value. So the starting point in any marketing exercise is actually **creating that value.**

Is it enough just to create value and sit back? How can you ensure that your prospective customers hear about the value you have created? How do you also ensure that others, such as your competitors, your business partners and the stakeholders in your eco-system, hear about your value differentiator? You need to **communicate your value** to them.

Now that you have communicated value to everyone in your ecosystem, will that make your products fly off the shelves? First of all, you need to make sure that your product is available on the shelf and second, you have to make sure that the product **delivers the value** that the communication has promised. Let's take an example.

You may have seen telecom service providers advertising on TV that a new service in downloading ringtones is launched and to be able to access these ringtones, you have to dial a number and follow the process that the IVR takes you through. If the process goes through without a hitch and you are able to download the ringtones of your choice, then the value that was communicated has been delivered.

Suppose after taking you through the whole process, just when you thought you could download the songs, the automated message says: 'Sorry! This service is not available in your city', how would you feel? Wouldn't you feel that what was promised was not delivered?

So it is important, not just to create value and communicate it, but also deliver what the communication has promised.

This is what marketing is: the whole process of creating value, communicating value and delivering value!.

In this Step, we will talk about how communicating value is ultimately for one purpose only – to firmly establish your product as a brand that your customers cannot live without.

I am not going to discuss what is branding or how you can build brands. I am going to focus on the things you need to do to make sure your product becomes a brand.

You've already guessed these brands, right? The brand names are not mentioned, and I know without a doubt that I could switch the colors, cover them partially or even invert these logos and you'll still guess the brands correctly. *That* is the importance of branding and building a brand identity.

Often companies, especially start-ups, forget that branding is an integral part of building the business. Entrepreneurs get so caught up with building the product, identifying the customer, looking out for funding options and building their team, that they tend to put things like brand name, logo, tagline, colors and collaterals – such as brochures, website, social media profiles – on the backburner. I have heard from start-up entrepreneurs that they will worry about these things when they have grown the business.

You need to focus on all of them from day one.

The first thing is the name. You cannot have a meaningless name simply because it sounds 'cool' or it's easy to pronounce. Preferably it shouldn't even be in a foreign language, because firstly, your customers might steer clear of your product because the name intimidates them. Secondly, it may be alien to your cultural context. A good name is one that rolls off the tongue easily, has relevance to its context, and invokes a feel-good association in you.

Let me give you a simple example of this. I have often been invited to business schools as a judge for their fests and all these fests have fancy, unpronounceable Spanish or French names. Last year I attended an entrepreneurial fest called *Antarprerna* and honestly the name was so inspirational in itself that I didn't think twice before accepting the invitation. I asked the organizers what made them choose that name, and the student who had come up with it said: "Because it is Indian and it is very relevant to the context of entrepreneurship." (*Antarprerna* is a Sanskrit word which means 'inspired from within'. All entrepreneurs necessarily have to be inspired from within).

You should choose the name of your brand with as much zeal and involvement as you would in choosing the name of your child. It has to have not only meaning and relevance but it should also never have the potential to embarrass you any time, now or in the future.

For example, don't call your training firm ABC Trainers just because that was the only thing you and your team could think of. Are A, B and C the initials of the founders? Or are your focus areas of business the A, B and C of training? If it is the latter, then you walk right into the trap that your competitors have set when they called themselves A to Z Trainers. Right? Another minor note, don't name your company with an X, Y or Z unless you simply *have* to. Because if there's a trade fair, your company will be listed right at the end of the directory!

Now that you have zeroed in on the name of your company, next in the order of importance is your logo. I have seen a number of entrepreneurs not realizing the importance of a logo. There's no sense in writing your company name in a fancy font with randomly chosen colors and calling it a logo. Logos are for brand recall. If you are a McDonald, even if people are driving at 140 kmph on the national highway, they should be able to spot your logo from miles away and pull up for a burger.

The key thing here is that your logo should be simple but unique. Simple enough that your customer remembers it; unique enough that even if your competitor copies it, yours will still stand apart.

Look at McDonald's 'M'; or Nike's swoosh; or Apple's half-eaten apple. There's no rocket science there. They are all simple, classy, and unique.

Also, your logo will be an integral part of all your collaterals. It is all pervasive – it is there on your visiting card, your letterhead, on your packaging, and on all your signage. Long, meandering, meaningless logos do nothing for brand recall. Short, relevant and crisp will.

Once your logo design is approved, you have to think about your colors. Colors have psychological importance. For instance, the yellow in the McDonald's logo is not by accident. Studies show that the color **yellow** stimulates hunger and it's also an eye-catching color.

Red is the color of life (because it's the color of blood). Therefore it stands for passion, energy, and excitement.

Blue has a cooling and calming effect. Usually spas and meditation centers will have an element of blue in their logos.

Green symbolizes nature and freshness, fertility and happiness. Hence green is often used for health and food products.

Put red and blue together and you get **Purple**. Purple is cooling like blue and powerful like red. It depicts royalty, knowledge, power and extravagance. Hence, luxury businesses will always use the color purple.

Orange depicts physical and mental comfort. It's a mixture of red and yellow and, thus, has features of both. Playfulness, youthfulness and energy can be portrayed through **orange**. Youth-related brands usually go for this color.

White is a reflection of all colors and it represents purity, precision, cleanliness and simplicity. Medical and health services or women's products usually use white.

Being the opposite of white, **Black** represents corporate culture, power, credibility and seriousness.

Pick your color depending on the emotion you want to evoke in your customer's mind when he thinks about your product.

Next is the tagline. This is not absolutely imperative but it's a good-to-have. A good tagline should not exceed 5 words – it could be a phrase or a brief sentence. It should be the perfect embellishment to your name. It should explain, and at the same time, it should cause a ripple of excitement in your customer. Café Coffee Day's tagline, for example, is 'A lot can happen over coffee'. It's self-explanatory and speaks wonders of their promise to their customer.

Don't fret if you can't think of one, right at the start of your business. You can even develop the tagline much later in your business depending on how your business evolves. For example, in our company CARMa, our tagline has changed thrice as the company has evolved in the last six months.

First it was, ***making every Indian an entrepreneur.*** It appealed to us because we are all passionate about making India an entrepreneurially vibrant nation.

Three months into the business, we said the services we offer are end-to-end and there is no one else who does the kind of things we do. So whenever people think of entrepreneurship, ours should be the first name on their lips. So our tagline became ***the first name in entrepreneurship.***

Then we discovered that the kind of services we offer, embrace a number of very different market segments and there is a whole stakeholder community out there whom we are trying to bring together, tap their synergies and create an eco-system. A habitat as it were, that is conducive for entrepreneurship. And lo and behold! Our new tagline is **building the entrepreneurial habitat**.

Now we come to the last aspect in branding – collaterals. These include visiting cards, brochures, fliers, presentation templates, and the website. You need to keep these collaterals ready, so you are able to create the necessary mind-space in your market segment and assetize it from the word go.

Remember this: Your collaterals are your prime real estate. You need to create them in such a way that they not only maximize yield for you but also effectively engage your market in such an intense conversation that it creates mind-barriers for your competitors.

Visiting Card

Your visiting card needs to be simply laid out and the elements that have to be included are: Company name and logo, tagline if you have one, office address, landline numbers, website url; your name, designation, email id, mobile number, and Skype handle. If you are an avid blogger, and your blog is about your business, it may not be a bad idea to include your blog id.

Your visiting card is prime real estate, so give it due respect. Do not crowd it with inconsequential details. Someone gave me a visiting card some time ago which had his Facebook, Twitter, Digg, and LinkedIn handles. I actually had to search for his name amidst all the clutter. You can include such details in your email along with your signature, if you are so particular, but not on your visiting card. If you have any AVs on You Tube, you can even provide links to them on your email. But keep your visiting card clean.

Please do not use your photograph on your visiting card. Perhaps it works when you are an actor, but when you are not, all it does is portray you as someone who is vain and self-obsessed. A young entrepreneur in Kanpur gave me his visiting card very proudly and drew my attention (not that I could have missed it even if I wanted to!) to the fact that, and I'm quoting him now: "I have put two pictures of myself ma'am, one in the front and one at the back, just to show how different I am. I did it even though it cost me so much!" I would have hurt him terribly had I said he was better off without his pictures at all, but what I mumbled instead was that the pictures didn't do justice to him!

Spend some time choosing the kind of card you want to use. Plastic and polymer cards are a complete NO because they are noteco-friendly and not cool. Use standard-sized cards because they are easy to carry and store. Custom-sized cards will also cost you more while printing. Please do not use scented cards. Someone once gave me a card that smelt something like a bathroom bleach and the damned smell clung to my fingers for days!

Use recycled paper. They show that you are green conscious but for god's sake, if you are in any business that contributes to carbon footprint, please stay away from using it, as it would not only seem like a travesty but a mockery too.

Let your card reflect your creativity without being over the top or in someone's face.

Make sure that the cards of the whole team in your organization have the same layout, look and feel. Recently I met two co-founders of a fairly successful company and both of them gave me their cards. The first thing that caught my eye was, in one the phone number was written as +91 987 654 3210. In another it was written as 9876 543210. It helps to understand the logic behind these phone numbers and write accordingly. For example, +91 is the country code, 98 is the service provider code, 765 is the area code and the last five digits are your number. So it makes a lot of sense to write it as +91 98-765-43210. Or you can club the service provider code and the area code and write it as +91 98765 43210.

Brochure

Your brochure needs to be a comprehensive document on your company, your product, the pain point it addresses, details of the founding team and your company's vision and philosophy. Don't try to cut costs by making a single-page incomplete brochure that will fail to excite and entice your customer. Take professional help while creating it. You don't have to go to large agencies to get your brochure designed. There are a number of young, bright, passionate and creative freelancers who do not charge you an arm and a leg. They will give you the respect that is due to you, and more importantly, they will give you designs on time without frustrating you. Pick someone you can work with on a long-term basis and not for just one job.

Some simple thumb rules while making your brochure:

1. If the page gets too wordy, provide relief intermittently with pictures. If you are using downloaded pictures from the net make sure you pay for their use.

2. Don't go crazy with colors like a kid with a new crayon box. Use colors meaningfully and judiciously. Stick to your corporate colors.

3. Also develop your own house-style when it comes to text. For example, all your text should be in one font only. Verdana, Calibri and Arialare good fonts to standardize. Make it a rule that all headers will be in font-size 14 and all text in 12. Make a choice between American English and British English and stick to it consistently (American is better because you won't have to deal with MS Office red-lining your British words! But as Indians, we are more used to the British style of English – we usually write COLOUR and not COLOR).

Fliers

Fliers are single-page documents that can be distributed or inserted into newspapers or put up at vantage points. You can use fliers for events such as exhibitions, launch of a new product, a new store, orthe addition of a new feature. The content on a flier needs to be crisp and interesting with contact, venue, and time details. The purpose of the flier is to grab your customer's attention in that split second before he trashes it. You could be selling an Apple product or ERP software. What matters are eye-ball grabbing, creative headlines.

Last and final is your website. Don't rush into this, and don't be petty while finding a good website designer. Your website can be the best interface for your customer, so never undervalue its importance.

In my experience, it is quite a challenge finding a good website designer. We went through three of them before we got what we wanted and in the process, wasted a whole year, not to mention a lot of money!. What I find surprising, is that there are more website designers than plumbers in a place like Bangalore but delivery does not seem to be their strong suit. So please do a thorough due diligence before you sign one on.

Once you have signed one, get your team into an isolated room and lock them in for the next 24 hours. Ask them to put down what they want in the website and why. All of us love a wish list but each wish has a cost attached to it. As a team you should all be able to thrash out why you need a website and what are you going to use it for. For example, if you are a manufacturer of steel furniture, chances are you need a website just as info-ware. You need to tell your customers who you are and what you offer. So the website will be nothing more than a web-brochure.

If, on the other hand, you are a company that sells high-end lingerie online, just a brochure-ware website will not serve the purpose. Yes you need to tell your customer about you and your product. But you also need to make it transactional so the customer can make a purchase online if she wishes to. Therefore, you need to create a payment gateway to facilitate online transactions.

Next, are your presentation templates. Standardize them. Unfortunately no school or college teaches you how to make presentations. Believe you me when I say, I have seen them all – bad, worse, and worst.

Your template should be in your house colors with your logo. It is not necessary to have your logo on every slide, but the first slide definitely should have your company name, logo, web url and tagline, if you have one. Choose a design which adds to the aesthetics, not diminishes it. And the design should remain the same through the presentation.

Your design should be unintrusive, so whatever text or picture you want to put up on the slide does not clash with the design.

Use a good blend of graphics, pictures and text on every slide. Make each slide look different, keeping the basic design the same.

If it is text, don't make it heavy by using huge sentences. Short bullet points not only lend to visual appeal but also ensure your audience pays attention to you. The bullet points should serve as pointers to you. If you have an essay on your slide, your audience may not know whether to listen to you or to read the slide. Usually, they end up doing neither and you have lost them.

Please don't use animation just for the heck of it. You need to animate *yourself*, your words, your body, your gestures, so they convey passion. Gimmickry does not make for a high attention span.

Don't go berserk with fonts and colors either. A clean background on a nicely-designed template, standardized fonts and colors, spatially well-laid out content accompanied by a well-prepared, well-rehearsed presentation, not only gets you customers but it will also go a long way in branding.

Lastly, I must talk about your grooming. Please remember, as an entrepreneur you are your brand's biggest asset and ambassador. However wonderful your product is and however passionate you are about it, it will not get you buy-in if you do the following things:

X Call your prospective customer from his reception and say: "I was passing by, so thought I will drop in on you to discuss my product!"

X Carry your presentation on a pen drive and ask your customer for his laptop. No way will anyone in his right mind allow a stranger to plug in your *god-knows-what-virus-it-has* pen drive into his system.

X Walk in half an hour late for a meeting and say: "Oh I was stuck in traffic!" Traffic is a fact of everyone's life and you better learn to factor it in yours too.

X Wear jeans that not only look unwashed but smell unwashed, with torn strands peeping from under your footwear.

X Wear round-necked tee-shirts with weird faces or slogans printed on them. I met a youngster whose tee had this message on the front: 'I am god!' And on the back: 'You are not!' I would have loved the tee if I was on a date with him, but considering he came to me for mentoring, I had to send him home to change into something more mortal.

X Wear socks with floaters/sandals.

X Go without using a deodorant, so much so, that the hapless prospect has to fumigate his office when you leave.

X I have a big peeve list when it comes to women entrepreneurs! They come in two distinct categories. One is the frumpy, visibly-harassed woman who is trying to meet me before her kid comes back from school. She has come straight from the kitchen, with telltale signs of breakfast on her *dupatta*, feet dragging heavily, a pair of flat, ugly, bathroom-slippers-like chappal, a shapeless *salwar kameez* shrouding her. Yes, she has an idea. No, she has no time. But she wants to 'do something'!

The other is the *uber* chic, accented, low-rise jean clad 'foreign' educated young woman who says she came back to India because India needs people like her yet in the same breath she tells me that her market is not India!

I think a sensible, educated, well-meaning (by that I mean someone who became an entrepreneur for the right reasons) woman is hidden between these two extremes and I'm seriously waiting for her to emerge!

> **TAKEAWAYS from step 15**

1. *Don't underestimate the importance of branding. Give it as much weightage as you would to other aspects of your business.*

2. *Brand recall comes from building a strong brand identity. A strong brand identity comes from doing all the right things in branding – brand name, logo, logo color, tagline and collaterals.*

3. *Personal grooming is as important, if not more important. Remember, you are your brand's biggest asset and ambassador!*

STEP 16

HOW DO YOU USE SOCIAL MEDIA
TECHNOLOGIES TO ACQUIRE
YOUR CUSTOMERS?

"HOW CAN YOU SQUANDER EVEN ONE
MORE DAY NOT TAKING ADVANTAGE
OF THE GREATEST SHIFTS OF OUR GENERATION?
HOW DARE YOU SETTLE FOR
LESS WHEN THE WORLD HAS MADE IT SO
EASY FOR YOU TO BE REMARKABLE?"

– SETH GODIN

Reaching out to your customer has three parts to it – acquiring your customer, retaining him and getting your customer to bring in other customers for you. Most importantly, how can you do all of this without spending an arm and a leg on advertising and brand-building?

Social media technology is an umbrella name given to social networking sites such as Facebook, LinkedIn, Orkut; to the blogs that people create on Wordpress or BlogSpotor micro blogs such as Twitter; to collaborations on wikis and open source for sharing content; to people reacting to each other through forums, rating and review sites; to organizing content by tagging them; and to special widgets that sit on your desktop and RSS feeds.

It goes without saying that all of the above use internet technology to power them.

We all know that people today use one or many or all of the above technologies for one reason or other. What we are looking at here, is how can you use them to reach out to your customer?

A couple of days ago I was invited to speak at the Biotech Park in Chennai for women entrepreneurs. There were eleven of them and most of them were post-graduates or Ph.Ds in biotechnology. Someone had set up a food-testing laboratory, another was making organic soaps, the third was creating monoclonal and polyclonal antibodies and so on. All of them said whilst they had excellent domain knowledge, their biggest problem was marketing. I asked them if they had tried reaching out to their customers using Facebook, or YouTube or blogs. They looked absolutely horrified and said: "No way! We keep scolding our teenage children that they waste too much time on them. How do you expect us to use them for marketing?"

Then I took them through a brief session on how they actually can use them and their horror turned to amazement and they said: "Can you please help us?"

Maybe these women are not-so-internet savvy and so they did not know how blogging can further their business. But I find it surprising when young, tech-savvy entrepreneurs, in the domain of internet technologies, allocate a certain budget for television and newspaper advertising! You are running a fashion portal and you are sitting pretty on prime advertising real estate, which is the internet, yet you want to be a dinosaur and acquire your customers through a process which is out-dated, expensive and unpredictable!

Internet is a double-edged sword. Its biggest plus is that it is viral and the message spreads like wild fire in nano seconds. Its biggest minus is that if the message is detrimental to you and your business, you are pretty much finished. Let me tell you a story to illustrate this.

You may have heard of a portal called Digg.com? Kevin Rose, a young entrepreneur started this portal a few years ago. He found great success and he was even featured on the cover of Newsweek. Digg.com allows its members to 'dig' any news story from anywhere on the internet, vote for it, or comment on it. If the story is not 'dug' by the members, it is soon 'buried'.

Sometime in April 2007, a blogger posted a comment that he had cracked the DVD code. Not only that, he even published the code.

Within hours of publishing this blog, Kevin Rose was threatened by an apex body in Hollywood that included such heavy weights as Sony, Disney, Microsoft and the like. He was asked to remove the link, pronto! Kevin Rose did, as he did not want to fall on the wrong side of those influential people.

Now two things happened. Firstly, even though Kevin Rose removed the link, the same had been picked up by other bloggers and by evening, there were several hundreds of them floating all over the internet.

Secondly, the customers of Digg.com were up in arms. They felt this was the best news story of the century. How could Kevin Rose remove the link?

Kevin Rose heard what his customers were saying and gave in. He put the link back on. And although the big guns had threatened him, there was nothing anyone could do as it was simply impossible to erase all the links from the internet.

Someone blogged saying, "Once something is on the internet it is hard to take it out, because 'you can't take pee out of the swimming pool'!"

Internet is a great leveller. Social media technologies have created the most democratic platform for your customers to voice their opinions, give their feedback, hear what you are saying. They can even partner with you to develop your products, evangelize for you and be your best buddy in the market place.

So why aren't you using them effectively to reach out to your customers? Look at the irony here. 8 out of 10 decisions in India to buy a car are made online, based on ratings and reviews in auto forums. Yet, I haven't seen too many car manufacturers active on these forums! What a lost opportunity!

You can find your prospective customers on Facebook or LinkedIn and customize your marketing message to them.

You can blog about your product, industry and your customers to stay connected with them and keep the buzz alive within your user community. Randy's Journal, a blog started by Randy Tinseth, VP of Boeing, is an excellent example of mobilizing customers by constantly talking about things that interest them.

NDTV Social, for instance, is a place where you can interact with your favourite anchors, newsreaders and presenters.

The 'Save Tiger' campaign on Facebook created awareness amongst millions of Indians on the dwindling tiger population and how it would harm the eco-system.

Do I need to say anything about the Anna Hazare campaign against corruption? It mobilized millions of people from across the country through Facebook, Twitter and SMS!

Tata Nano was launched with constant updates on Twitter.

Pepsi's new advertising campaign, which is endorsed by actor Ranbir Kapoor, actually allows users to chat with him on Facebook!

You all know Sunsilk's famous gang of girls campaign.

Even to this day, it is to www.espncricinfo.com that most cricket aficionados turn to for cricket score updates even as a match is in progress.

These are a few examples of how new and even traditional businesses are using social media to connect with their customers, acquire new customers and maintain high-decibel mind-share with their user community.

Let me also warn you that by just opening a Facebook account or becoming a member of LinkedIn, you cannot mobilize your customers. It is a strategic tool like any other and you should use it with discretion and a lot of planning, for it to become effective. My recommendation is that you partner with an agency that will manage your marketing for you, using social media. There are a number of them in most Indian metros and it is good to work out a retainer-based model with them. Some of my mentees have very effectively partnered with them by working out a small-fixed and high-variable 'success' fee model.

In Bangalore, you have Alive Now, Catalyst Labs, Geek; in Chennai you have BYT Social, Echovme, D'Zine garage; in Mumbai you have Drizzling, Communicate 2.0, Bcebwise, Experience Commerce, Flea Global, FoxyMoron; and in Delhi you have Strat, New Media Guru, OMLogic. Many of these have offices in multiple locations as well. For a full list of the top 50 agencies that deal exclusively with social media technologies, check out www.soravjain.com/2011/01/indian-social-media-and-digital.html

As I said earlier, you have a wide array of options to choose from when it comes to social media technologies.

Use a simple thumb rule before choosing what works for you. Ask yourself these questions:

✓ Is it going to enable a new way of connecting with your target market?

✓ Is it easy to sign up?

✓ Is there a distinct power shift in that control now vests with the individual and not the institution?

✓ Is it an open platform?

✓ Can you, by using it, build a perpetually interested and locked-in community?

Choose whatever works for you. Blogging, tweeting, you tube-ing, flickering, sns-ing (sns =social networking sites), RSS-ing (feeds that are sent out to your customers) rotten tomatoing (movie review site), delicious-ing (where you can bookmark your favourite sites on your browsers) .You name it and you have it. Think of them as your business strategy tools and use them effectively.

The other day, in a pub, I heard the best pick up line from a fellow drinker: "Hey, you look familiar. Have I met you on twitter?!"

> **TAKEAWAYS from step 16**

1. *Social media technologies, when used effectively, can be the best way to reach out to both your prospective and existing customers.*

2. *Social media is free and your customer acquisition cost therefore is very low as compared to traditional forms of media like TV and newspapers.*

3. *Use social media technologies judiciously. Don't be trigger happy and update your profile for the sake of it. Your customers must see some value in what you are communicating to them.*

4. *Never use the internet to bad-mouth a competitor. News spreads like wildfire and you will be squashed even before you know what hit you.*

STEP 17

WHAT IS YOUR INNOVATION PIPELINE?

"ALL TRUTH PASSES THROUGH
THREE STAGES.
FIRST, IT IS RIDICULED.
SECOND, IT IS VIOLENTLY OPPOSED.
THIRD, IT IS ACCEPTED
AS BEING SELF-EVIDENT."

- ARTHUR SCHOPENHAUER

Innovation is the foundation on which businesses are built. So if the foundation is not rock solid, the organization you build will also be wobbly.

I have gone through several business plans which are built on one idea, catering to one market, with one way of reaching that market. Let's say everything goes according to plan, and you are able to swamp the market. The ride lasts for three years. In the meantime, other players who have seen the opportunity have also come into the market. Because they came in later, they have made sure they don't make the same mistakes you made. Not just that, they have also made sure they offer a compelling reason to your customers to leave you and go to them.

What are you going to do then? Many entrepreneurs caught in such a situation behave like deer in headlights. Panic, and quickly come up with a knee-jerk strategy. Typically, the easiest thing to do to hold on to customers is drop prices. This will bring you some quick relief, no doubt. But you will realize how temporary a solution it is, when your competitors offer not only prices significantly lower than yours but also exceptional product value. Who do you think the customers will go to then? Don't forget in today's context, market dynamics have changed so much that customer loyalty is as fleeting as a shooting star. (Wow, this sounds so much like Navjot Singh Sidhu!) It takes years and years of painstaking innovation to build customer loyalty.

A young mentee of ours manufactures automotive abrasives. He competes with some real heavy weights in the industry. In a very short span of time, he has managed to acquire customers who swear by him. How did he do it? Not just by offering good quality products but also customization, flexibility and total value-for-money prices.

Recently, one big player in the industry decided to flex his muscle and offered the same customer way lower prices than what our mentee was supplying at. Now the customer was in a dilemma. He called our mentee and said: "I love your product. I love the fact that you listen to us and deliver the way we want. But the fact remains, I have no way of justifying why we continue to pay higher prices to you when a well-established player is offering the same product to us at really low prices. I don't want to lose you, so can you do something about it?"

Our mentee came to us in panic and said, "I cannot afford to lose this customer. I have no choice but to drop my prices. But if I drop prices, my margins will shrink badly and I can't afford that either!"

We helped him with a strategy which did not include dropping prices. And that strategy centred on innovation. The innovation was not just about adding value to his product but his customer's as well and he was able to demonstrate to him why it made economic sense to stay with him.

This was possible because our mentee had a robust innovation pipeline. One of the things investors look for in a business plan is, firstly, whether there is a clear road map for innovation, and secondly, whether there is a clear monetizing plan for innovation. So the way it works is, you go to market with one product, one market segment and one way of delivering value, but pretty much on the back of it, there are other ideas in the pipeline to delight your customers, add value to your engagement with them, and make them hungry for your products. This makes your innovation pipeline the biggest entry barrier to your competitors.

Innovation is not a good-to-have. It is not even a must-have. It is not even a cannot-have. It's not a choice that you make. You don't have the luxury of choosing whether you want to innovate or not. When you become an entrepreneur, it should come as easily and naturally to you as breathing in and breathing out.

There are many myths that abound innovation. The biggest myth of the mall is that you have to be innovative only in the start-up stage. I usually tell my students, you have to be innovative till **you** die or **your company** dies. This is non-negotiable. A successful entrepreneur is one who not only has 'innovation thinking' capability in him but who has also fostered a culture of innovation within every level and layer of his organization. Let me share an excellent example of innovation thinking.

After World War II, most of the fish on the Japanese seashores were either dead or contaminated, thanks to the bombing of Hiroshima and Nagasaki. The fishermen had no choice but to go way into the sea to catch fish. The only problem was that since it was far from the shore, it took them a while to travel back, set up shop on the beach and sell the fish. In the meantime, the fish would lose its freshness and the customers refused to pay good prices for them.

The fishermen then came up with an innovative idea: Why not have freezers on their fishing boats? It seemed like a logical solution at that time. The problem was that customers said frozen fish does not taste as good as fresh fish, so they will still pay lower prices.

The challenge now was, how do you keep fish fresh despite the distance? Again, the logical answer seemed to be to keep them in their natural habitat, which was water. They removed the freezers and added fish tanks. But they'd pack the fish tanks so tight with fish that there would be no place for the fish to move inside the tank. If they can't move, the fish become sluggish and lose freshness. The customers said these fish don't taste the same as fresh fish, hence we will pay lower prices.

This is where the common sense leads to game-changing innovations. One of the fishermen said, "Let's put a well-fed baby shark in the fish tank. It may eat a couple of fish but that's fine." Now the fish do not know that the shark is well-fed, so they scramble all around the fish tank to escape the shark. Their continued activity keeps them fresh!

The customers were delighted with the fresh fish and paid a premium price for it.

Simple and sensible thinking on part of the fishermen led to an innovation which addressed the customer's pain point effectively.

The second myth is that innovations have to be earth-shattering. Something like a Hiroshima and Nagasaki. It is not necessary that all innovations should be like the Wright Bros ones or should have as far-reaching an impact as Edward Jenner's. Such big ticket innovations probably happen a few times in a century and if mankind was to be dependent on such rare occurrences, we wouldn't have made any progress.

Also, the internet has made it possible to innovate constantly and incrementally. With just a little tweaking, you can now have an altogether new business model for an altogether new market segment. Look at Bharat Matrimony for example. Murugavel, who founded the company, started it off as a simple matrimonial portal and look at how many product iterations and innovations the site has spawned? Many competitors like the Times of India's simplymarry.com also entered the market, but none has been able to break Murugavel's stranglehold on the market.

The third myth is that innovation is only with respect to product. Product innovation is certainly a huge aspect of it but is not all of it. We have seen how you can be innovative in pricing, in packaging, in delivery, etc., in Step 13.

My submission to all entrepreneurs is to never underestimate the power of innovation as a strategic tool. Look at Facebook for instance. Mark Zuckerberg has just announced that his company will enter the computer hardware market as, "We found over time that a lot of the stuff that the mass manufacturers put out wasn't exactly in line with what we needed and what other social apps needed".

Zuckerberg has teamed up with HP, Dell, AMD and Intel to launch the 'open compute project' to create the technical infrastructure that will power Facebook which has more than 30 billion photos, videos and other content shared by users, month on month. This is a fantastic strategic move on his part to not only make his site more efficient but also to open a new industry for all the social networking sites, which will in turn draw new customers every day.

Innovation is also an instrument of empowerment and transformation. In India, both the PM and the President have declared the current decade as the 'decade of innovation'. The areas which need disruptive innovation to transform lives are agriculture, health, education, water management, and infrastructure. Disruptive innovation means developing and deploying radical, inclusive, sustainable and home-grown technologies using community knowledge and wisdom, local culture and native raw materials.

The Honey Bee Network in India promoted by Prof Anil Gupta, of IIM Ahmedabad, has done exactly this and they have managed to mobilize 140,000 ideas, from 545 districts of India!

Pranav Mistry's 'SixthSense', which he developed at MIT Media Lab, is an amazing tool that connects natural hand gestures to the physical world through the digital information it generates. More than his innovation, what I found most endearing was what he said on TED, that he wants to go back to India and use this innovation to dramatically improve the lives of fellow Indians!

Gone are the days when people could be labelled into three separate boxes: Scientists, Academicians, and Businessmen. In organizations today, all three either are rolled into one or all three need to come together to create successful innovations. No one today enthuses only about how many patents have been filed. Everyone wants to know how many of those patents have gone to market successfully.

Innovation pipeline puts you firmly in the driver's seat and no competitor can pull a surprise on you. Look at what is happening in the world of tablets. When Apple launched the iPad, it was 13.4 mm thick. The iPad2 is 8.8 mm thick. So thin that you are scared to hold it in your hand for fear that it might just slip through your fingers! Can you believe it? 8.8 mm thick means it is even thinner than smartphones!

Even before the world recovered from this shocker, Samsung launched two more tablets, with Android 3.0 – a 10.1-inch and an 8.9-inch Galaxy tab, a few weeks ago at the CTIA Wireless 2011 show in Florida. Just a month before that, Samsung unveiled a different 10.1-inch tab at the Mobile World Congress. It seems that all the while Samsung had several mind-blowing products in its innovation pipeline, to pull the rug from under Apple's market!

Like I said before, innovation pipeline helps you not only be market-ready but it also helps you surprise and delight your customers, time and time again.

> **TAKEAWAYS from step 17**

1. *Innovation is the only constant in today's volatile, ever-changing market.*

2. *Go to market with one product; focus on one market and freeze on one way of reaching out to that market but keep your innovation pipeline buzzing constantly so you take your competitor by surprise. Not the other way around.*

3. *Innovation need not be only product-based.*

4. *Innovate or perish should be not just yours, but also your entire team's mantra.*

WHY DO YOU NEED
TO THINK 'GREEN'?

"PERFECTION IS ACHIEVED,
NOT WHEN THERE IS
NOTHING MORE TO ADD,
BUT WHEN THERE IS NOTHING
LEFT TO TAKE AWAY."

- ANTOINE DE SAINT EXUPERY

I have the good fortune of being a Mentor with New Ventures India (NVI), Hyderabad, a joint venture between World Resources Institute, Washington, and CII–Sohrabji Green Business Centre (CII-GBC), Hyderabad. NVI promotes clean-tech entrepreneurship and it is housed in the CII-GBC building, which was the greenest building on earth when it was built in 2003. It was also the only Platinum-rated green building outside of USA.

I must share an interesting incident that happened when the building was under construction. Since it was decided that the CII-GBC office would be a green building, it meant, using building material that was eco-friendly, ensuring the architecture was LEED compliant and so on.

Keeping this in mind, the purchase team went shopping for floor and wall tiles and they were obviously looking for the "greenest" ones. They were hard to come by those days. In every store they visited, the shopkeeper was eager to show them the best tiles that he had in stock which were all imported from Italy, finely polished, etc.

In one of the stores, the purchase team was surveying the yard, attached to the store. It seemed to have a lot of 'junk' material and they accidently stumbled upon a big, unsold pile of tiles covered in dust. On enquiry, the shopkeeper sheepishly admitted that those tiles had 20% recycled material and he had therefore made no attempt to sell them.

Much to his chagrin, the purchase team chose to buy the unwanted lot and those are the tiles that you will see today in the CII-GBC office in Hyderabad!

There was a time in human history when people assumed that if a machine made loud noise, it was state-of-the-art. It was considered a sign of growth if big chimneys bellowed the darkest of smoke. The bigger and more fuel-guzzling the car was, higher the status of the person owning it.

How times have changed. Now we proudly display our business cards that are made of 100% recycled paper. Owners proudly flaunt the fact that they used fly ash bricks in construction of their house/office. Some time ago, I personally bought an electric two wheeler even though it was not particularly cheap, because I felt it was green.

Noise and environmental pollution are not only looked down upon now, but they also cost you money, and in some cases, they may threaten the very survival of the business itself.

My business partner Hemant told me about a flourishing industrial area in the Bidar district of Karnataka. A few decades ago, there were a number of pharmaceutical companies, manufacturing units and the like, that did not plan for the waste disposal and environmental pollution they were causing. 90% of these businesses have now shut down, as they could not comply with the mandatory pollution norms. The ongoing cases on Lavasa and Adarsh are examples of environmental impact that businesses have to consider.

So, what is green preparation? Why has it become necessary? Who should do it? And, how do we do it? Let us look at each of these points one by one.

What is Green preparation?

The new mantra of today is "accelerating growth, preserving ecology". It is no longer a slogan, no longer a cool thing to do and no longer a moral responsibility. It has become an imperative. Every business has to think green to future-proof itself. The legislation may require you to do it, business consideration may force you to do it and the customers may demand it of you. So what is it?

Being 'green' means you are expected to respect the environment around you – use minimum water and energy; waste least amount of resources; recycle what you can and so on. In other words, you can think green in everything that you do – your business, products, team, and raw material, the waste your business generates and where your products end up after use. You are responsible for all this. One popular way to measure your green credibility is by measuring your complete Carbon Footprint. There are professionals who can help you measure the same.

Why has 'green' become necessary?

The world human population has exploded from 3 billion in 1960 to 6.9 billion in 2011. Add to this, is the fact that the requirement of each human being has multiplied and the natural habitat cover has drastically come down to make way for human settlements. Energy and water are becoming issues like never before. Energy has already caused many wars and international posturing. Last year, I was at a Chief Minister's Conference and one of the bureaucrats was complaining that the power situation in Bangalore had worsened and there were more hours without power than with. One of the Chief Ministers said that in the coming years, power will become a non-issue as water shortage will make us re-think the way we live. True, enough, in many of the metros, we have already begun to see evidence of this.

Nations are looking at securing energy, water, and bio-diversity very seriously. It is becoming imperative for all businesses, big and small, to be 'green-aware' and sustainable from day one. Sometimes you may be forced by the legislative requirements to comply with green norms, and at other times you may be forced to become green to meet the market demands.

Who should do it?

We live in such an interconnected world that national boundaries are no longer barriers for trade or impact. So you may be small, big, important, or inconsequential. You may be a student, a rag-picker, or a beggar. You may be selling product or service. You may be butcher, baker, or candle-stick maker. It does not matter. As long as you are alive and living on this planet, you do have a Carbon Footprint to your existence and, hence, every individual has to think, plan and act 'green' for himself and for his business.

How to be green?

Now that we all understand the need to be 'green', the next question is what exactly do we do to be green?

By its very nature, brick-and-mortar businesses have greater Carbon Footprint than internet businesses and hence have greater responsibilities. The former should professionally plan to be green right from the drawing board stage.

For internet businesses, in absence of any particular bench mark, I would suggest that until your business reaches a top line of ₹ 1 crore per annum, you prepare to be 'green' from your internal planning. Once you cross that, get professional help to do a Carbon Footprint mapping. This will allow you to know where your environmental impact is most and, thus, help you plan the initiatives specifically in those areas that will make you green.

Greening your manufacturing facility

Factories source raw material from various locations, employ large numbers of people and ship the products to various destinations. The broad guidelines to become green are to look at all activities from end to end and try to comply with the green guidelines.

Broadly the focus should be on the following:

- Go for Green Factory Ratings. They will help you design your factory in such a way that it utilizes optimum units of power, water and other resources.

- While sourcing raw material, you need to consider if it is a renewable source, and from where it is transported to reach your factory.

- How much waste is generated in your manufacturing process?

- How power intensive is the manufacturing process?

- What packaging material is used and where does it come from?

- How far is your market from your production base?

- What happens to the leftovers after your product is consumed by the end user?

- What means of transport does your staff use to reach the workplace?

- What transport do you use to reach your products to the market?

- What kind of clothes does your staff wear?

- What kind of food is served to your staff in the cafeteria?

As you can see, you can and should think green in every single area.

Greening your internet business

In my experience, I have seen technology businesses becoming 'green' complacent because they neither use any raw materials nor do they have a manufacturing facility. Hence, the assumption is that their green impact is low. Nothing could be farther from truth.

The Carbon Footprint study conducted in a large consulting organization recently, brought out some stark facts with respect to how they had not been very 'green' in their business. The areas they identified where they could definitely go green were:

- Paper used for printing

- Transportation of staff to the workplace and to other places for work reasons.

- The energy consumption on air-conditioning and lighting.

- The very building they worked in could be retrofitted to become green.

Once they identified these areas, it became easy for them to make small changes, which in turn brought in a significant reduction in their carbon footprint.

Thinking green and acting green not only gives you brownie points but also makes perfect business sense. Go Green!

> ### > TAKEAWAYS from step 18

1. *Going green is no longer an option but a mandate.*

2. *If you are unaware about how to go green or what is your businesses carbon footprint, get professionals to help you.*

3. *Both internet businesses as well as manufacturing can easily make changes to go green.*

4. *There is no sense in creating a large business, if there are no people left to enjoy the offering!*

BUSINESS
INCUBATOR

STEP 19

WHY ARE INCUBATORS NEEDED IN COLLEGES?

"FIRST THEY IGNORE YOU,
THEN THEY LAUGH AT YOU,
THEN THEY FIGHT YOU,
THEN YOU WIN."

- MAHATMA GANDHI

I have been teaching entrepreneurship and mentoring entrepreneurs for the last six years. Since I am a traveling teacher, I have had the opportunity of teaching in a number of business and engineering schools. My students are from diverse backgrounds, they have different aspirations and mind sets. My observations based on my experience are:

- There is a greater awareness about entrepreneurship in metros and some of the business schools have even included a course in entrepreneurship in their MBA program.

- The more branded the business school is, the less it encourages entrepreneurship. Its brand equity comes from placements, not from how many students in a batch become entrepreneurs.

- The tier II and tier III towns are hungry for exposure but there is neither a full-fledged course in entrepreneurship nor are there competitions and events which are entrepreneurship-centric.

- The schools that offer entrepreneurship think that this is like any other management subject and can therefore be taught theoretically. Whenever I see a chapter with the heading: Role of Entrepreneurship in economic development, I gag!

- In some of the business schools, they have even asked me to set three sample question papers and I have tried in vain to explain that they cannot treat this course the way they treat the others.

- I have also seen that in some schools, entrepreneurship started off as an elective subject but it has now become a compulsory one.

- Engineering schools have not yet felt the need to introduce a course in entrepreneurship, although in some universities they have a management paper in which a chapter on entrepreneurship is included.

- The interesting thing is in some engineering schools, management is taught by any teacher who is inclined to do so, never mind that his subject is mechanical engineering!

- In most places, entrepreneurship is taught by management professors who have never been entrepreneurs.

- No entrepreneurship course teaches you the importance of mentoring.

- There is a notion that an entrepreneurship course is only for those who want to become entrepreneurs. It is important for schools to propagate that in today's extremely competitive job market, employees who have 'intrapreneurial thinking', that is, those who take ownership of the road map, even if they don't own the business, have a distinct edge.

- Nowhere in India have I seen the course linked to an incubator.

The simple truth is, in India, there are very few incubators. Nor is there any awareness of the imperative of incubators. This is why, very few students become entrepreneurs.

Incubators are a must in tier II and tier III towns as, entrepreneurially, these are under-served areas. It is my firm belief that in the next five years, India will see game-changing ideas and trail-blazing entrepreneurs coming out of Meerut, Guntur, Salem, Rajkot, Hubli, Siliguri, Puri, Aurangabad, Nagpur, and the like. Incubators will make sure this actually happens.

What the incubator should provide?

The five most important components of an incubator are:

1. A 20-hour course in the basics of entrepreneurship

2. Mentorship

3. Seed/pre seed capital

4. Support services (accounts, legal, statutory)

5. Real estate, necessarily in that order.

Basic course in entrepreneurship

This course is designed to expose students to the basics of entrepreneurship. Real-time entrepreneurs from different domains and in different phases of growth should be invited on an interactive platform to share their journey, their highs and lows. They should talk about the mistakes they made, the lessons they learnt and their vision. The subjects covered should include psychological preparation necessary for becoming an entrepreneur, the process of ideation, how to choose and validate ideas in the market place, how to estimate resources, how to put a face to your customer, what are the funding options, how to transform yourself from a peer into a leader, the need for an innovation pipeline, how to develop revenue models, and how to write the business plan. At the end of the course, students should submit business plans and the best of the business plans should be incubated.

Mentorship

Very few incubators provide mentorship. Mentorship is about bridging the experience gap, as I have already talked about. Today more and more youngsters are becoming entrepreneurs right out of engineering and management schools. They have no exposure as to how organizations function, so obviously they have no clue about how to build organizations that function effectively. This is where mentors play a crucial role.

Mentorship is also about networking. As a young entrepreneur, the only thing he has going for him is the twinkle in his eye, the passion in his heart and the song on his lips. He needs someone who is in a position to open doors for him.

Mentorship is about knowledge. Ask any entrepreneur whether he knows how to build the business around his idea, and the answer will be an emphatic no. Right from writing the business plan to incorporating the company to filing for patent to hiring the right team to going to the market fully armed and doing all the right things at the right time, it is the mentor who will hand-hold him. A mentor is a must-have, not just a good-to-have.

Pre-seed/seed capital

Very few incubators provide capital. Many entrepreneurs need money to develop prototypes. No investor funds prototype development and not all students have the ability to fund it. A good incubator should provide this. Unfortunately even in international conferences, I have heard professors from ivy-league schools lamenting that they are not able to encourage entrepreneurship because the institution does not have funding. What use is an incubator without seed fund? The incubator may start with a corpus of ₹ 2.5 million.

Going forward, the fund can be made into a sizeable corpus by leveraging alumni network, roping in international funding agencies that are interested in leaving a footprint in India, partnering with international agencies specifically interested in the clean-tech space, or high-social impact projects, central and state government grants, etc.

Support Services

The key areas where incubatees need support are legal (company incorporation, statutory compliance), intellectual property protection (filing for patent), and accounting (bookkeeping, payroll). These should be offered to the incubatees by partnering with a good accounting and legal firm.

Infrastructure

Some educational institutions comply on the real estate bit. They provide work stations, computers with internet and telephone. Many of them charge a rental for it.

Debt or Equity?

The college can either take a stake in the company for all the mentioned services it provides or it can offer it as a loan, payable with interest at the end of two years when incubation ends. If it is debt and the incubatee returns the loan with interest, the money can be plowed back into the corpus.

Could have, would have, should have.

The most irrefutable reason for having an incubator, in engineering and business schools in India, is that it takes away regret from the ideating populace. Good incubators give the necessary push and thrust for ideas to come forth and see the light of the day. In the absence of incubators, many an idea is still-born.

> **> TAKEAWAYS from step 19**
>
> 1. Incubators in colleges are must-haves.
>
> 2. Incubators are the only way to ensure that a conducive eco-system is created so that good ideas actually reach the market place.
>
> 3. Business schools and engineering colleges must open their eyes to the need of the hour – setting up incubators, encouraging entrepreneurship and shooting the placement officer, not necessarily in that order!

STEP 20

WHAT IS 'SOCIAL ENTREPRENEURSHIP' ?

"EVERYTHING HAS BEEN FIGURED OUT,
EXCEPT HOW TO LIVE."

- JEAN-PAUL SARTRE

Recently I was invited to speak at a global conference on 'The business of business is peace'. That's where I first propounded my anti-gravity theory on social entrepreneurship. It's not exactly Newtonian but it adds just the right touch of erudition to my street speech!

Stripped of all rhetoric, my theory is simply this. For years in India, the political powers that be, have propagated that in human society there is a natural imbalance. There are haves and there are have-nots. The haves are a small minority and the have-nots, of course, are both rabid and rampant. It is the job of the haves to generate surplus and distribute it to the have-nots who will in turn remain servile forever and ever in the face of such unbridled generosity. And that is how it will always be because that is how it always was.

Why are there some who have and others who don't? Oh, that is because of Karma and sins of past life visiting upon this life, etc.

This state of affairs has been passed on from generation to generation for centuries. Barring a few episodes of unrest and revolt in history, the status quo has been blissfully maintained.

In the post-liberalization era, the new shibboleth was the famous 'bottom of the pyramid' and how there was a silent consumer revolution waiting to brew at the bottom of the pyramid. We were also told that MNCs which 'discovered' the bottom of the pyramid were laughing their way to the banks and how consumerism has arrived with a big bang in India.

All I have done is mixed both these realities and produced a new cocktail. Suppose the bottom of the pyramid was exciting, not because there are masses of 'consumers' hidden under the rock, but because there is a whole community of 'producers' who, with a little mentoring to give them access to resources and markets, are able to build significantly profitable businesses and generate surplus. Suppose this community flips the old model on its head and instead of surplus wealth percolating downwards as charity, you not only generate surplus at the bottom but you also let it bubble to the top of the pyramid, defying gravity?

I have actually seen this happening with the women I mentor in Afghanistan, Ethiopia, Somalia, Nigeria, Ghana and India. These are illiter ate women who became members of micro-financed clusters, looking for a way to put two meals on the table, for themselves and their children. They were ordinary people engaged in very ordinary activities at a basic sustenance level. It is a textbook case of livelihood entrepreneurship.

Never in their wildest dreams did they envision a scenario where they would transform themselves from livelihood to opportunity-based entrepreneurs. Never did they factor in a possibility that one day they would contribute to the GDP of their country and how!

This is the new language of empowerment. The women are not on dole. They collaborate to produce, market, and make money in the most laissez-faire kind of way. They are driven by the market forces of demand and supply, governed by the most basic of economics – you produce to market, you market to profit and you profit to generate surplus. This is my new theory of anti-gravity of social entrepreneurship. It is not a business model which rests on passing the hat around, or keeping the women 'occupied' or basically perpetuating the exploitative state of sustenance and livelihood entrepreneurship, which maybe a tad better than being jobless, but below the poverty line it is, nevertheless!

The reason for my including this step on social entrepreneurship the way it is and the way it should be is that many of you come to me saying you want to be an entrepreneur and you want to be, more specifically, a social entrepreneur. Although you all tell me that you want to become a social entrepreneur because you want to do good to society, the sub-text that I hear is that you want to build a not-for-profit model that creates livelihood at the grassroots level. Because it is not-for-profit, it has to be fuelled by charity, grant and largesse!

The bottom of the pyramid needs access to resources and markets. Not benevolence

The bottom of the pyramid needs to become a beehive of producers. Not passive consumers.

If that access is denied either willfully or out of ignorance, believe you me, you have a mutiny in the making. We have already seen evidence of it in terrorist acts, in Naxalism, in vandalism. Earlier it was natural to see a sky-scraper and a clutch of slums, rubbing shoulders. The slum-dwellers looked upon the skyscraper dwellers as their subsistence creators and therefore even looked up to them. The skyscraper dwellers needed the slum inhabitants to run their houses, as their maids, cooks, gardeners, drivers, launderers and dog-walkers came from there. So there was amicability, even interdependence of a sordid kind.

Times have changed. The slum dweller no longer accepts that it is his past karma that is keeping him grounded. He is demanding equal opportunity to produce, profit and prevail. If this opportunity is denied, he will, wily nily go grab it and if in the process there is a surge of violence, so be it. Let's not forget that 26/11 seared though our collective souls because for the first time terrorism entered penthouses and upper-class drawing rooms.

Without meaning to exaggerate or terrify, I'd like to end it by just saying this: Inclusive growth is not a good-to-have, but must-have. Inclusive growth is possible only if you have forward thinking entrepreneurs. Inclusive growth is possible only if more and more of us become entrepreneurs. If we remember inclusive growth only at the time of election, don't be surprised if your maid's son is the next Kasab!

> **TAKEAWAYS from step 20**

1. *Don't become a social entrepreneur if you are on a high moral ground and you want to do 'good' in society without generating profit.*

2. *The purpose of social entrepreneurship is to transform livelihood entrepreneurs to opportunity-based entrepreneurs. This means that they will produce, generate surplus and that surplus will make its way up the pyramid.*

3. *Remember, inclusive growth is the only way forward.*

Let's Fly!

"How much more there is now to living! Instead of our drab
slogging back and forth to the fishing boats, there's reason to life!
We can lift ourselves out of ignorance, we can find ourselves as
creatures of excellence and intelligence and skill.
We can be free! We can learn to fly!"

– Jonathan Livingston Seagull

Hopefully by now the book has helped you do all the right things to start
your company, create your product, and take it to the market. Now discover
the joys of flying even as you watch your product fly off the shelf!
We will meet again so that I can take you through all the steps of growing
your business!

BOOKS THAT I WILL TAKE TO MY GRAVE!

1. Personality not included – Rohit Bhargava
2. The Art of the Start – Guy Kawasaki
3. Tribes – Seth Godin
4. Purple Cow – Seth Godin
5. Groundswell – Charlene Li and Josh Bernoff
6. Brain rules – John Medina
7. Reality check – Guy Kawasaki
8. Creating customer evangelists – Ben McConnell
9. The power of myth – Joseph Campbell
10. The act of creation – Arthur Koestler
11. The social psychology of organizing – Karl Weick
12. The tipping point – Malcolm Gladwell
13. The outliers – Malcolm Gladwell
14. Chaos – James Gleick
15. Collapse : How societies choose to fail or succeed – Jared Diamond
16. Naked Conversations – Robert Scoble and Shel Israel
17. The black swan – Nassim Taleb
18. Biz as usual – Christopher Locke
19. Surely you're joking, Mr Feynman – Richard Feynman
20. Cracking creativity – Michael Michalko
21. A short history of nearly everything – Bill Bryson
22. The man who mistook his wife for a hat – Oliver Sachs
23. Understanding computers and cognition – Terry Winograd and Fernando Flores
24. Metaphors we live by – George Lakoff and Mark Johnston
25. The ten faces of innovation – Tom Keeley
26. Creativity games for trainers – Robert Epstein
27. Made to stick- Chip and Dan Heath
28. Blue Ocean strategy – W Chan Kim
29. Crossing the chasm – Geoffrey Moore
30. The long tail – Chris Anderson
31. The game changer – AG Lafley
32. Copyrights and Copy wrongs – Siva Vaidyanathan

PROFESSOR NANDINI VAIDYANATHAN

She's a travelling teacher who teaches entrepreneurship in several ivy-league business schools around the world. From being just a word in the dictionary five years ago, it has now consumed her whole being.

Her moment of epiphany happened four years ago when she realized that in India not too many people became entrepreneurs simply because they didn't know how. So she founded her company Startups to mentor entrepreneurs (forstartups.blogspot.com). Up until July this year, she has mentored over 500 startup entrepreneurs across domains, across geographies, pro bono. Twenty years in the corporate sector, in MNC's on all inhabited continents, have given her enough reason to say, been there, done that.

Startups has also been involved in mentoring women, at the bottom of the pyramid, to become opportunity enterprises creating surplus and generating enormous value. Startups has mentored over 6500 women in economies as plural as Afghanistan, countries in South and East Africa and India.

A year ago, she co-founded CARMa (Creating Access to Resources & Markets), (www.carmaconnect.in) with a lofty ambition: to change the karma of entrepreneurs in India. CARMa mentors startups, mature enterprises and family businesses. The mentoring encompasses getting organizations investment ready, creating business excellence and shortening the learning cycle of entrepreneurs in India.

She writes a regular monthly column for the magazine, Entrepreneur. It delights her no end that it is from smaller towns that aspiring and practicing entrepreneurs reach out to her after reading it.

She is a TED speaker.

She lives in Bangalore (although she travels 300 days a year!) with her daughter, Medini and their dog, Mocha.